UNCOMMON SENSE:
VISION FOR A NEW AMERICA

ADDRESSED TO THE
INHABITANTS
OF
AMERICA

~

GEORGE ROLLAND WOLFE

~

*For my parents, Skip & Joan,
to whom I owe too much to say.*

*And for my wife, Thea,
whose ideas are so intertwined with mine
that it's too much to parse.*

Contents

§

*Transparency - Rule of Law - Taxation -
Education - National Service - Campaign Finance -
Debts & Deficits - Political Parties - Healthcare -
Local Defense - National Defense - Environment -
Immigration - Firearms - Voting - House of
Representatives - Senate - Executive - Judicial -
Constitutional Convention*

PREFACE

For those of you who don't know or have forgotten what Thomas Paine did with his pamphlet, Common Sense (January, 1776), you're not alone. Originally conceived as a series of letters, it grew in scope and ended up being one of the most popular booklets in American history. It's not frequently referenced these days, however, even with all the civil unrest and other disruptions that 2020 has thrown at us. Along with a second popular pamphlet (American Crisis) published in December of that same historic year, Paine sought to rile up his fellow Americans on behalf of the cause for independence from England. The ultimate goal was to achieve liberation and, if possible, create a radical new system of self-government. Common Sense was the initial call to action while American Crisis was a cry to keep the faith (in light of how dreadful the war was going at that time). I thought it was fitting to revisit Common Sense in particular, due to the historic events of 2020, which seemed to have parallels to 1776. "Uncommon sense" struck me as what would be necessary to get beyond the many impasses of government that we currently face.

I am not a historian, a political scientist or a Constitutional expert—just a guy who, like most Americans, simply wants a level playing field and a functional government we can be proud of once again. To me though, we don't have a shortage of experts; rather, we have a shortage of will, vision, and ability to enforce our existing laws that regulate government.

It's my hope that this booklet will help to shift those elements, create necessary discussions and ultimately lead to action on any of the subjects contained herein.

G.R.W. July 4, 2020

INTRODUCTION

§

Abuse of power once again arises in America, this time not from a foreign power such as England but from within: our own administration. Having it always within us, however, to reinvent our individual self, I believe we must now look to reinvent our collective self—our government—and thus, our world, as a means to protect ourselves from such abuse once and for all.

The sickness, which has swept over the land, is at such a fevered pitch that we can scarcely breathe. The events in Minneapolis, spread through protest from sea to shining sea, and now beyond our shores, were a match to a bonfire, built up over the course of a months-long lockdown, years of despair, decades of unfulfilled promises of liberty and equality, and centuries of heartbreak, persecution and suffering.

Amid curfew from these days of uprisings against the brutal treatment of our fellow citizens, we find ourselves in a country no longer experiencing domestic tranquility nor the blessings of liberty. They are replaced instead with the chill of disillusionment and the sting of injustice amid a glaringly imperfect union.

These are, once again, "times that try men's souls."

Knees upon our necks, we're forced to recall the days of the Boston Tea Party, when the overflow of emotion, and taxation upon the patience of the People, provoked their wrath, led to a bloody revolution and, ultimately, birthed a unique form of government to the world.

Though we do now still see our most cherished amendments

holding strong — freedom of speech, of the press, of religion, of the right of the People to assemble peaceably (mostly) and petition the Government for a redress of grievances — we are forced to entertain doubts. We see our rights today, but will those rights live long enough to see tomorrow?

The cause of America is still the cause of all mankind: whether a people can responsibly govern themselves. Our state of affairs is now of universal concern, as "the principles of all lovers of mankind" which still guide us, are now sacred to many more countries than we had in the days of our founding. Our compatriots are no longer simply the People of America but the Peoples of the world who embrace true democracy, equality and the fundamental human rights of men, women and children. In a time of extreme uneasiness, there is yet comfort and peace in this.

But whether this Republic can withstand the constant pressures that threaten it — the solid blows and a thousand cuts — is yet to be seen, though, some will assume this is assured. Empires, by their nature, come to an end. Our story is not yet completed, so our destiny is, rightly, a matter of great conjecture and contention. We are either at the beginning of the end or at the beginning of a whole new era.

Our Constitution and our natural rights are under attack from all sides. It is now upon us, a new generation of patriots, to raise our voices, take a stand and ultimately strengthen the democratic foundation of our Nation.

Resist division, bring forth those better angels, and unite, regardless of faction, to rid this tyranny from the face of the Earth and recreate the best possible government.

— **G.R.W. Los Angeles, May 30, 2020**

CHAPTER 1

§

On the Need to Recreate Government

Amid this great pandemic and economic collapse, we are experiencing a test upon our instruments of government, the likes of which we have not seen before.

As the executive branch increases its war with the states, as whole departments of government do battle, as key officials are hauled off to jail only to be released, as foreign powers hack our voting systems, as demagogues rear their heads, and as warring parties reach new partisan extremes, the People despair at this corrupt state of being.

Even health itself divides us: To shelter in place or venture out? To mask or not to mask?

We have reached another crossroads in our history. But let us use this moment as an opportunity to perform a time-honored duty: to perfect the form of government that our founders began. We are called upon to recreate government from time to time — the goal being to keep it effective and relevant to the changing issues of each day and age — and right now such a time has come again.

"The tree of liberty must be refreshed from time to time with the blood of patriots and tyrants. It is its natural manure," noted Jefferson in a letter. "What country can preserve its liberties if their rulers are not warned from time to time that their people preserve the spirit of resistance? [...] God forbid we should ever be 20 years without such a rebellion."

Others, like Sam Adams, were equally adamant that we not shy away from confrontation at times when it is demanded of us. "If ever a time should come, when vain and aspiring men shall possess the highest seats in Government, our country will stand in need of its experienced patriots to prevent its ruin."

Adams had a talent for needling people to action, "If ye

love wealth better than liberty, the tranquility of servitude than the animated contest of freedom — go home from us in peace. We ask not your counsels or arms. Crouch down and lick the hands which feed you. May your chains sit lightly upon you, and may posterity forget that you were our countrymen! [...] If we suffer tamely a lawless attack upon our liberty, we encourage it, and involve others in our doom."

Why shy away anyway, for we have it in us. Was it not in our blood, when justified by a tyrannous foe to lash out, to tar and feather, to loot and fill Boston Harbor with the salty tea of the British Empire? We tore down statues of the King. Once again, it's high time for toppling.

Did we not upend a country and fight a bloody Civil War to defeat the curse of slavery? These are the growing pains of a worthy cause.

Did we not put bodies in harm's way a hundred years from then, to try to end a system of oppression that had more than run its course? These are the milestones of deliverance.

It is in the nature of all disheartened countries, such as ours at this time, that it can be said: "rioting is the language of the unheard."

Oppression against one of us is oppression against all, and it must not stand. Why hide behind the notion that this is not our fight? If one of our colonies had voiced a grievance against King George for an injustice, how would the other colonies have reacted? Would they have said: "this is not our battle" and that they, themselves, are not the victims of tyranny? No, they aligned with those unfortunate brothers to whom the wrong was visited.

Likewise, we cannot afford to let ourselves, the People, become divided. Be stronger, more resolute and smarter. Meet force with force and do not allow creeping injustice to sink its roots into fertile soil. Hold the line and do not fear to take to the streets, to the capital or wherever else justice is demanded.

Keep to the issues that bind us as a people — these common

things are far more numerous than tyrants would have you believe. If tyranny is revisiting our doorstep, then we must find it in ourselves to rise up and strike it down.

There is little time for mincing words and small acts of dissent—these will not rebalance the high crimes that have been committed. There is no time for incremental change—that ship has sailed; in fact, it has sunk. Our battle and calling is that of a taller order: It is the high road, a grievance of a people against the reckless corruption of a broken state.

Our fight is that of an aggrieved People against generations of wrongs, of countless sins that do not fit the reputation of a great power—it is that of a nation committed to fulfilling its solemn vows to fix what is now broken, to suture that which has been severed.

Do not suffer fools in the highest echelons of government or incompetence in the marbled halls of power. Do not suffer the depravity and treachery of morally bankrupt leadership, bent upon denying democracy and everything that's been sacrificed in the name of America.

In this spirit, when we again feel the despair of our fellow citizens, and when we realize the value of what is dear to us only as it is threatened, let us be compelled to better understand how we arrived at this precipice. Perhaps only then will we gain the wisdom to know the proper actions to recreate government—something new forged from elements of the old.

Brevity & Truth

Another founder, Thomas Paine, began his famous treatise with the urge to draw from "a principle of nature" that "the more simple any thing is, the less liable it is to be disordered, and the easier repaired when disordered."

It's fitting that our Constitution is likewise known for its terse economy, with succinct articles, rights of man, and ensuing amendments—even as that compression has perhaps left too much room for misinterpretation and exploitation.

Perhaps we still have an inkling of this brevity in us, too, even at this later point in time.

So let this experiment, too, be marked by such condensation. I will strive, then, for a comparable truth, terseness and transparency, with a nod to our most aspirational founding papers.

In Light of the New

Savvy as they were, our founders could only see so far forward in the attempt to solve for future generations, which they were deeply committed to.

They did not imagine the armies of pundits, anchors and networks that grease the machinery of modern news entertainment.

They could not imagine the influence of new technologies — radio, TV, Internet — as they intersect with politics.

How could they imagine the creation and spread of lobbyists, political action committees and think tanks that dull and confuse the ears of our public representatives?

They did not imagine whole new industries and subjects, like public relations or political science.

They could not imagine the growth of public representatives into career politicians.

There are benefits to many of these things, yet along with them go many aches and pains that are now the source of so much angst, dissent and strife.

What would our founders say now about this current state of affairs?

In their day they saw a country living in infancy. They rightly identified our nascent potential, as has now come to pass.

Thomas Paine yearned for a great navy to traverse the oceans. He hoped America might use its abundant natural resources to create an armada to rival and surpass those of France, Spain and even England herself. It is done.

George Rolland Wolfe

Our founders would be surprised to see that our former adversary, England, is now our closest ally. But the lines of sovereignty are now firmly drawn, and there's not the slightest suspicion that the monarch would impose herself upon America's will, leveling unfair taxes and tyranny, and quartering troops throughout our communities — these problems are now leveled at us from within our own country, as the mayors of our cities have taken up the task of removing unwanted federal troops.

Our founders would likewise find comfort in the Nation's economic might, whose fortune has grown by leaps and bounds, beyond their wildest imaginations. We have established our central bank, now tested and adjusted through two and a half centuries of trial and error. We have established our central leadership, now a string of forty-five presidencies unbroken in succession — even if not all have been of sound mind.

Certainly these are signs that our founders' impulses, their instincts, were right, at least in the broader strokes of the pen and aspirations to sovereignty. But more than two centuries of live experimentation with their proposed system has also brought forth confounding contradictions.

An enduring Constitution, blueprint for a budding government, still steers us. Though imperfect, it is represented by a Congress with, arguably, enough checks on power to have gotten us to this point. A respectable Judiciary, arguably, inspects and rules on our laws.

In this so-called "workshop of Liberty to the Civilized World," we have not only succeeded at the American experiment in government, but now that same notion spans the globe by the hundreds, spawning the goods and furnishings of democracy — even improving upon them — and quickening the pursuit of happiness and the insurance of general worldly welfare, wherever liberty finds safe harbor. Even if we were to fail, the seed we have put forth into the world would likely succeed in its original aim of establishing in the world a new self-governing structure.

Our founders would find comfort in an America that is not only home to its own seat of government, the United States, but by its leadership on the world stage has formed a governing body in a United Nations, providing a balance among nations, aspiring to keep wars at bay, and global economies moving efficiently and in harmony. Pay no attention to our ability, however, to embed the control of that deliberative body to a few elite nations with special privilege.

And all this, now 50 states from just 13 disparate colonies, from the mere twig of a country on the cusp of oblivion, even in its crib. Truly, incomplete as it is, America's mere survival was a long shot over these 250-odd years. An admirable achievement, yes, but at what cost? We don't generally like to consider such unpleasantries.

Other countries like Italy, Greece and Egypt evolved over millennia, but America's rapid aging, its vaulting rags to riches tale, sets it apart. Perhaps we are now seeing the flies in the ointment of such sudden evolution.

We have grown in might, tripling the combined armaments of the next most armed nations, yet our weaknesses were revealed when we could not prevent a group of hackers, halfway across the world, from influencing our presidential elections.

We have grown into the wealthiest nation, yet we have the highest rates of imprisoning our own people.

We have grown into one of the most unequal countries in the world, in the gap between rich and poor — ironic for a country that began with such lofty notions of equality.

That America has been, at least until this current period, a leader that the rest of the world could largely look up to with honor and respect, and could expect to hold to high standards, a place of principled values and fair play, would've been a strange reality in the days of our founding. At the time, the crux was whether we could be seen in the eyes of the established world as a stable place for the investment of capital; now we are very much the embodiment of capitalism.

America has not only survived, but has been a force to be reckoned with—one that helped defeat or rein in formidable armies and powers on the world stage: the Nazi Tyranny, the Soviet system, and many other forms of oppression. And yet, a curious trait of our personality is in our ability to perform these incredible feats while simultaneously oppressing significant portions of our own people.

That America developed the means to put a man on the moon would, of course, be unfathomable to our founders, let alone that our tiny inventions, these communications now in each citizen's pocket, would have many times more power than those giant rockets.

Yes, we should celebrate what is deserving but not be haughty. Let us also be chastened for reaching such heights while still not having secured fair representation for all our people. We should not bristle at such notions and simply retreat into arrogance, for we have work to do in further securing the necessary checks and balances of government. The current state of the union points not just to our successes but also to our shortcomings.

Our founders would have found little comfort in our current crisis. Their marveling at our subsequent achievements would have soon be tempered by the sight of their greatest fears coming to light: the empowerment of a demagogue, the meddling of foreign powers, and the paralysis of partisan politics. At the same time, their efforts to preserve the power of elites by keeping the masses from having too much control have largely succeeded, through the excessive powers of the Senate, and the Executive branch via the electoral college.

On Preserving Liberty

It is doubtful, however, they would agree that preserving liberty meant hiding it somewhere—as if in a mason jar in a cellar—so that it would never to see the light of day, never to be reworked and perfected.

Yet this is how we treat our Constitution.

Now comes the chance, though, to break the jar and release Liberty anew.

The movement toward ever-greater Democracy does not mean putting our minds in the frame of those who, though brilliant, lived without the information we now possess.

These men, eminent as they were, would encourage us to use all means at our disposal to right the wrongs they could not solve, to solve the problems they could not fathom, and to fathom a path that leads to a successful conclusion.

They did, for instance, embed safeguards to ensure the survival of the system they put in place, but we have seen many of these escape valves erode over time. The electoral college failed in its appointed role to override the 'mobocracy,' allowing an autocrat into power and causing great damage to the Republic. And the Senate, supposedly the older and wiser brother of Congress, was complicit in the destruction of our values and institutions. The Supreme Court, too, in their 2013 gutting of the Voting Rights Act, and by inserting big money into political campaigns in their Citizens United decision (2010), has played a key role in undermining democracy.

Our founders did not give us the benefit of the Constitution with the expectation that we should limit our thoughts and knowledge. After all, it was their insatiable curiosity and incessant questioning that led them to succeed where other Republics failed.

Certainly, they would have wanted us to keep the spirit of their intent, but adapt and grow with the times.

We know from their words and actions that they encouraged the periodic re-creation of government, as evidenced by their transition from the Articles of Confederation to the Constitution and beyond, with amendments and the gradual evolution of our laws.

Even beyond our founders, other leaders, like influential Supreme Court chief justice John Marshall (1801-1835), echoed this same sentiment of flexibility to new circumstances and evolving values: "...a constitution, intended to endure for ages to come, and consequently, to be adapted to the various crises of human affairs."

There is no good to come from only looking backwards, to the original words, for that merely calcifies a period of Colonialism in the modern world. This stance is merely a thinly veiled cover to run from the brave fulfillment of our grandest promises.

This is the challenge before us. Our founders put great value in their words, but they also expected specific results to come from those carefully chosen words. Now is the time to take up the task of improving their work and making sure their words aren't just empty catchphrases but that they actually mean something substantial. They were a forward-looking group who thought in uncommon ways, and we need to think in similar ways whenever we reach such epic impasses. They decided that the original Articles of Confederation weren't quite doing the job of running the new Nation, so they pivoted and wrote the Constitution.

Our modern symptoms of government failure and debilitation are glaring. It has been nearly 50 years since we had a substantial amendment to the Constitution: the 26th Amendment, in 1971: the right to vote for those who've turned 18. That doesn't sound much like responsive government. All the while, our debts and deficits edge upwards, unimpeded, seemingly infinite. Yet there's nothing to address that but business as usual. We have developed systemic and widespread problems with some of our most fundamental practices, such as the basic notion of fair voting. But we sit silent, paralyzed.

I will delve into these issues, and many others, over the course of this pamphlet—and even then we will barely scratch the surface of what must be done. Still, albeit imperfect, we do what we can.

Manifesting Destiny

Thomas Paine reminds us that: "Tyranny, like hell, is not easily conquered; yet we have this consolation with us, that the harder the conflict, the more glorious the triumph. What we obtain too cheap, we esteem too lightly."

Indeed, too many of us have grown up with a relatively secure government as a given—but we're quickly discovering that because of this, we've valued it too cheaply. Every now and then we're called upon to seize the day and raise Hell for things we hold so dear, for they wouldn't be dear if not for the fight.

Haven't we waited long enough to finally ensure Happiness and Tranquility for not just some of us, but all our People?

Let us manifest a destiny that fulfills our Original Promises in the Declaration of Independence and our Constitution;

Let us manifest a destiny for a True Democracy of America and Her People, finally;

Let us manifest a destiny for our rightful place in a world where peace on earth is real, and tyranny is forever vanquished.

Will we now, facing down tyrants, hesitate when we see the whites of their lies? Let us not delay, but take the fight to them today.

CHAPTER 2

§

America's Original Sins

We must face our original sins — Genocide and Slavery. So many promises we've made but never kept; so many treaties we've signed and then betrayed. From the beginning, we have been a people of lofty morals and dirty deeds.

So many massacres we've brokered, from Napituca to Wounded Knee, and people cut down, from Mangas Coloradas to Sitting Bull.

We are a people of broken Promises. Is that what we want as our legacy, what we want our grandchildren to know about us? Or can we pivot and save our Nation's soul?

No credible history or substantial inspection of America can be complete without a proper accounting of our deepest secrets and an honest appraisal of our fundamental structures.

We have spoken plenty of America's power. We have related Her exceptionalism, but we must now confront the things we do not speak of.

We may yet become a People who rise up and correct themselves, make amends and ask the hard questions. But to succeed we must ask forgiveness and restore pillaged Justice and Democracy.

So much meaning we've attached to race, though it's nothing but a fabrication of men, its conception undermining our greatest ideals.

We must speak of all the letters of the alphabet that now have a long list of names attached, those who died unjustly: Ahmaud Arbery, Breonna Taylor, Michael Brown, Rayshard Brooks, Philandro Castile, Medgar Evers, Eric Garner, Fred Hampton, George Floyd and so on.

We can no longer keep faceless that which we must now

face. For what good are all our sanitized history books, whitewashed with half-truths and half-baked mythologies of flawless heroes?

This country was founded on stolen lands, baptized in the blood of native peoples, its economy established upon the backs of African slave labor, its industrial railroads built with the toil of Chinese laborers, and its cities raised by an endless stream of immigrants.

It is time for us to come clean.

For what good can come from a People so fragile that they cannot even look themselves in the mirror to see the full and honest truth?

Let us cease to conceal who we are;

Let us be transparent, and by so doing cast out our demons;

Let us confront our truths, and if a Great Reckoning must be, then so be it. If we succeed, then may it usher in a new American Revolution.

Are we a People who bury our heads in sand?

Are we a People who descend from the cowardly mob of night riders, only too happy to hide behind masks?

We must be better than that, before the world answers "yes" to all of the above.

We have spoken of America's resourcefulness, Her creativity and innovation, but we must now drop all that if we are to find our better selves and continue to evolve as a country.

Great nations do not shirk or slink, for it is in the degree of transparency that their greatness resides. We have played this game of denial with our past for more than 500 years.

We owe it to future generations to look deeper, to know better, and to reach the heights of virtue to which we aspire.

This is no way for a great power to lead. We cannot wither at this critical stage, shy of realizing our potential, our promise of equal rights for all.

We must gather the courage we felt in our revolutionary struggles — at Bunker Hill, at the signing of our Declaration of Independence, at Valley Forge — and use that kernel of spirit to sculpt a new future, endowed with integrity.

We are a people who pride ourselves on personal responsibility, yet we refuse to face up to our sins. If there is a time to pull ourselves up by our bootstraps, this is it.

As a people who pride themselves on freedom and liberty, what better way to pay homage to our past than to free ourselves from these great burdens, once and for all.

Let us move on to a new America, cleansed by a bonfire of truth.

Let us uplift a Great Spirit of a better America.

What We Did & Do

We acknowledge that racism caused, and continues to cause, irreparable harm to countless people, families and communities, and has too often split the country in two.

We acknowledge the Middle Passage of the slave trade, the early days of plantations, the Civil War and its painful aftermath, the years of Jim Crow terror, the Red Summers and the Great Migrations — and all else resembling these things, too numerous to name.

We acknowledge the culpability of the North as well as the South, with New England mills and New York bankers likewise profiting immensely from slave labor. It is no underestimation that we built an empire on the backs of free labor — corporate welfare in one of its earliest and most grotesque forms.

We acknowledge the hundreds of sundown town purges and all the race massacres.

We acknowledge all the slain individuals and leaders, being

too many in number to fairly honor, and all those who suffered and sacrificed for the Civil Rights movement.

We acknowledge the evil perpetrated by all the laws that enabled and legalized murder. We acknowledge the hazy wording of the 13th Amendment and the legacy of slavery it kept alive through mass incarceration.

We acknowledge the rescinding of the order to grant 40 acres to freemen and all the obstacles put in the way of owning land and growing capital.

We acknowledge the failure of the Freedman's Bureau and other federal institutions, unable or unwilling to stop racial injustice that took back towns, cities and whole states.

We acknowledge the failures of too many Presidents and Congresses, those who pulled support for free men, women and children everywhere, allowing seeds of hate to spread and grow anew.

With regard to the unfathomable suffering of Native Peoples across the Americas, we acknowledge that countless atrocities — and genocide — have caused, and continue to cause, irreparable harm to individuals, families and tribal communities.

We acknowledge the 5 to 15 million indigenous people who were here in 1492, at the arrival of Columbus, and the fewer than 250,000 who remained by 1900 — a loss of more than 9 out of every 10.

We acknowledge the pain that came with nearly 400 treaties, most of them a string of broken promises.

We acknowledge the suffering of the Trail of Tears and the executions at Mankato. We acknowledge the myriad massacres, from Florida to California.

We acknowledge the incessant wars, attacks and raids upon Native tribes. We acknowledge the disease-riddled blankets gifted by settlers, and the California Genocide.

We acknowledge the policy of Assimilation and the taking of children, and the reeducation and brainwashing, all to impose our will upon another people. We acknowledge the policy of Termination and the efforts to unrecognize indigenous people out of existence.

We acknowledge all the persecuted or slain leaders, being too many in number to fairly honor. We acknowledge legal injustices across generations and from century to century.

We acknowledge the deceit that took away ancestral lands and desecrated sacred spaces. We acknowledge the failure of the Bureau of Indian Affairs and other institutions, unable or unwilling to stop the endless stream of tribal injustice.

We acknowledge the failings of far too many Presidents and Congresses, those who pulled support for Native Peoples, allowing the continued spread of hate and neglect; the response has been inadequate at best and deadly at worst.

Repent & Divest

Whether our go-to words, like "freedom" "liberty" and "equality," are our bond is yet to be seen.

Do we care enough about the integrity of our words or shall we simply slur them until they are unintelligible, meaningless grunts? Are we the type who breaks his word so much that he loses all credibility with those who still value integrity and the rule of law?

It is never too late to change our words and our ways. Let us find it in ourselves to take a stand on behalf of the pursuit of Happiness, and Justice for all, and realize Martin Luther King, Jr.'s dream — that is, the unfulfilled American dream.

We know we have it within ourselves. There is time yet to make good, but we are running out of such opportunities. The real question isn't whether we can do it, but if we can muster the will to do it.

A first step on the road to Justice must be a candid accounting, a truth and reconciliation akin to what was witnessed in South Africa. For let us be honest:

If we were not such a powerful country, more powerful

countries would boycott us and divest of our wrongful ways and unbridled greed.

If we did not write the history ourselves, as a conquering people, we would more closely resemble the villains we so detest in our own tales.

If we did not conceive and rule among the select united nations of men, we might well find ourselves on the receiving end of crimes against humanity.

Is it too late to reconcile? No. To reconcile is to bow down, but bowing down allows for the possibility of rising up again, even stronger.

Is America too proud to reconcile her past to her present? What would we ask of our children if they were to commit a wrong? — so it should be with us.

Divest, America, of bigotry and bile.
Divest, America, of prejudice and perfidy.
Divest, America, of malice and malignancy.
And let Freedom truly ring.

American Crisis: Democracy v. Capitalism

Our economic system, too, bears some responsibility for our past transgressions and our current predicament.

With occasionally brief periods of respite, we have largely chosen capitalism over democracy.

We saw this in the steadily increasing quest for capital, instead of relationships, that has driven most of our history. We saw it in the search for gold, for land, and other resources that came with all our westward expansion. There were forests to be felled, railroads to be built and people to be conquered.

Our founders, still crafting systems of government and fledgling economies, could not have foreseen the collision of capitalism and democracy that we now see.

But capitalism and democracy cannot survive as equals; one must always dominate. If we are to live in a democratic society, then capitalism and all it entails must be regulated to favor the people. If we choose a capitalist society, then we must be prepared to put democracy aside, in favor of the corporation—now declared a person with natural rights—who will want to have his way.

With slavery, capitalism won out over people: it drove the business of human capital for more than a hundred years.

The Industrial Revolution offered a glimpse into how askew things could get between the haves and the have-nots. As capitalism moved naturally toward monopoly, its excesses were addressed and it was curtailed in favor of the people—for a time, at least. But the "Roaring '20s" put an end to that.

The Depression, then, shook faith in our economic system and forced us to focus once again upon the People. We continued to recover and build ourselves up. But it wasn't long until, by the '50s, we reached the point where even the president had to warn us about the dangers of unchecked greed—in that case, the "military-industrial complex."

The '60s and '70s briefly reminded us of the importance of our relationships to others.

But in the ensuing fifty years or so, up to 2020, the damage by corporations, beyond their connection to our military, has become increasingly apparent. This has happened because we have ceased to be a particularly "alert and knowledgeable citizenry."

The fallout can be seen in the fundamental inequities of the People, a schism that increases at an exponential rate:

While Main Street suffers, with 10% or more of the workforce unemployed, Wall Street prospers by leaps and bounds. While Main Street suffers and Ma and Pa shops go bankrupt, Wall Street celebrates the triumphant return of business amid the pandemic. While Main Street suffers, with so many people now living in tents and shanties, Wall

Street rides new highs. While Main Street suffers, with a pandemic raging that has killed more than 200,000 of our own people in its first seven months, Wall Street brags of newfound confidence and exuberance. While Main Street suffers, and the government answers by adding trillions of dollars of debt, Wall Street cheers a never-ending ascent.

Gone are the days when monopolies were reined in. Gone are the days when a solution to our debt was not so easy as simply printing money. Gone are the days when the People had more say, more power, than the Corporation.

As Capitalism impinges on the promise of democracy, our dreams get deferred and remain unfulfilled. Our still-struggling democracy is failing against the overwhelming force of capitalism run amok.

And yet, conversely, the same political instability that diminishes democracy also threatens capitalism, as discontent and protests emerge, and people reevaluate their fundamental relationships, including with corporations. If the People become so impoverished, and the middle class continues to shrink while corporations grow stronger, at some point capitalism may cannibalize itself. There will simply not be enough consumers with sufficient capital to buy what corporations are offering.

To rebalance our democratic systems of government and focus on the People again, perhaps we need to divest of ourselves — that is, selectively, of our own corporations — to force change.

Capitalism in America, like our government itself, is badly in need of restructuring. There must not only be a democratic reckoning and reconstruction of government, but also an economic reckoning and reconstruction.

A New Dawn

And yet, despite the doom and gloom, I believe a New Dawn is breaking over America.

CHAPTER 3

§

Allegiance

Many of our current problems of law and government stem from America's longest war — the Civil War, now nearly 160 years long and counting.

The "Lost Cause" — the ideology that the South's Confederacy is still a noble venture — is fitting: as with Islamic extremism, it shares a near cultish obsession with loss and martyrdom. Both movements are concerned with holding onto outdated, overzealous and hateful traditions that fly in the face of a rapidly changing world, and core American values.

These adherents have built their dissent and terror brand around the Confederate flag, though they are now more dispersed beyond the South, to all states.

"The principle for which we contended," said Jefferson Davis after the South's defeat, "is bound to reassert itself, though it may be at another time and in another form." The Union may have won the war, but the United States has been battling the same adversary ever since — and that has exerted a large toll on us as a country.

The Civil War, being about slavery, was converted to a battle over "state's rights."

"The foe now was central authority and national will," writes historian Jon Meacham. The war shifted from the battlefield to politics, as Confederate sympathizers extended their influence in D.C. and westwards as the country grew. "We have taken up new hopes, new arms, new methods," wrote one of the their chief proponents, Edward Pollard.

Jim Crow laws spread, budding black power diminished and terrorist groups roamed freely. There is no allegiance here to the United States wherever members of the Lost Cause reside — there is only elaborate window dressing. There is just the tedious urge to hate in brand new ways. Today's faux Republicans—those complicit in the current administration's agenda—have pushed for changes that are in sync with Lost Cause efforts, such as: voter suppression, mass incarceration of people of color, gutting the federal government, stacking the Judiciary, denying healthcare or job equity to minorities, and using private militia to quell democratic protests.

There is no allegiance here to the Nation as a whole, no matter how hard these people may wave the American flag. These are enemies of the United States. The oath of all public servants is created for this purpose: "...to defend against all enemies, foreign and domestic..." But what are these strategies and plots except domestic terrorism by another name?

As a person cannot logically worship two gods, people cannot worship two flags: that of the Union and that of the Confederacy. No matter how much talk there is of "preserving heritage" through their flag, or statues, or whatever else is the foil, the attempts are just another way of trying to continue the oppressive ways of the Old South.

These adherents must join the Union—the United States—and reaffirm their loyalty, taking an oath that they are no longer aligned with a power opposed to it, or they should find another country to live in that supports their beliefs.

If an American citizen can't agree to this, then why should we allow their continued presence in this country? They can either adapt and pledge allegiance, or go back to wherever they came from.

Allies

With regard to our natural democratic allies in this day and age—other democracies—we seem to squander the power of this potential alliance. Once we've dismantled the antagonistic elements among us, we must align ourselves anew with our protagonistic elements around the world.

Nearly 60% of countries with more than 500,000 inhabitants are democratic; only 13% are considered predominantly autocracies; the rest are a type of hybrid along the spectrum. In

George Rolland Wolfe

1976, democracies represented just 25%. All in all, despite our gripes about the loss of democracy in the world, "Broadly speaking, the share of democracies among the world's governments has been on an upward trend since the mid-1970s, and now sits just shy of its post-World War II record."

Granted, each country must fend for itself with its own policies, and its borders dictate what can happen within it. But it is to our collective advantage to join together more often, and to preserve and expand our international democratic force rather than allow ourselves to be divided and disempowered.

Think of our combined democratic assets as a labor union, and our buying power and our sheer numbers as our leverage. We're not talking merely about the global economy; this is about the people connecting with like-minded people, and steadily becoming a solid alliance through better communications and bold actions.

It was a shock for Americans to think that George Floyd's murder could elicit a global response. We didn't know there was so much of a sense of shared humanity for a problem that seemed limited to the United States.

It was surprising to see the South Korean K-pop bands mobilize and overload social media tags used by opponents of Black Lives Matter. We didn't know what this fan base could see in something that appeared to be a uniquely American issue, but it was enormously gratifying that they became valued allies to the protest movement.

We could seize on examples like this and learn to negotiate from the strongest possible position on many other important issues. Such an interconnected force could position itself as speaking for the mutual interests of its international members. It could use that weight to improve the world's conditions and other benefits for humanity that could result from such alliances.

As with our founders, we have the chance to strengthen the natural rights of world citizens — rights that transcend individual country barriers. These are things like universal freedom of the press, religious freedom, gender equality, environmental standards, and impartial judiciaries in the court of world affairs, among many other issues we could tackle.

We are no longer just "the People" but rather "the Peoples." We can take heart in this subtle but substantial shift in thinking, and double-down on our efforts to ally ourselves with all who support true democracy.

The world did this quite well when it came to applying pressure upon the tyrannical government of South Africa during the 1980s. The Peoples of the world decided to divest their capital from companies that did business with South Africa. Over time, businesses were forced to listen. Students protested on their campuses and got their schools to divest their endowments of any corporations that dealt with South Africa — until change happened.

May we no longer just reflexively fight against strife and wars. Let's think bigger. Let us strategically develop a prominent voice with which to shape the world.

The State of the Police

When my fellow citizens have spoken of fear of government, I would usually tend to declare it an overreaction, a sign of a paranoid mind. "The fear of government is not something relevant to our time and place," I'd think, "but rather an event of our distant past, when kings and queens ruled the day."

But now I've seen how easily a single voice — say, a president — can twist the course of a well-meaning country. By signaling support to meet protests with unchecked brute force ("when the looting starts, the shooting starts"), it was clear how this encouraged violent actions on the part of the police — those whom we have entrusted with our safety.

Why have we, the People, given over such powers only to see a police state arise in our midst, our police, turn so violently against the very people who seek and expect protection? What instructors and managers are there who would create such a culture? When did the "good guys" switch sides?

All cops are not bastards, but we do have a problem — a big, complex problem to solve.

Why have we, the People, paid such sums to our leaders, our mayors, only to see a police state learn new means by which to control the People? How is it that such a system has been given militarized weaponry inappropriate for their narrow calling? Why have we, the People, not seen the daily abuses so clearly perpetrated upon our fellow man as we do now? How blind can we be?

But as the powers of the police state derive from the People, it is now time for the People to withdraw, at least in part, those overarching powers. If the police and their unions cannot police themselves, then how could they possibly, police the People responsibly? If the police cannot police themselves, the lack of which has become all too apparent, then how could they ever be trusted by the People who are—never forget—their employer?

In what other line of business would it be permitted and normal for an employee to turn on his employer, raise his hand against him, and injure or strike him down, then expect to return to work as normal without repercussion? And yet we accept this insanity as normal.

It is not the job of the People to worry about how to behave so as not to upset a nervous officer of the law. It is the officer's job to earn the respect of the People, every day, or to find some other employment befitting his temperament.

Nor is the job of the People to fret about how they should behave such that anyone feels they take their lives into their hands when they leave the house, stay in the house, or deal with the police in any way whatsoever.

It is not right, and it should not be tolerated, that the People be stripped of a fair chance to present legal grievance to, and criminally hold accountable, those whom they have, essentially, appointed and entrusted to these positions of power.

This is not a police worthy of our trust. This is not a police worthy of our funds. This is not a police worthy of our Country.

Those elements, the countless barrels of bad apples that have infiltrated and debased the police, must be rooted out.

Serving as an officer is no job for the ignorant, for anyone who can fog a mirror—no, the role of the police is sacred. It must be filled by a highly select and rigorously trained and battle-tested group of the People; these should be among the best of the best, in the realm and spirit of the best of our teachers, who truly care for the interests of the People.

Unchecked authority, immunity, is no longer acceptable, as with police unions. Be officers of the Peace, or do not be officers at all. The People can give, and they can take away.

Our bond of mutual understanding is to secure the general welfare of the People. Those whom we have employed in worthy and respectable jobs have broken a sacred bond.

The events which began in Minneapolis have reverberated like the shot heard 'round the world. We see how they would so shamelessly press their knees upon the necks of all Americans.

Have they forgotten their oath to serve and to protect? Have they lost their minds as they beat with batons and pepper spray, and shoot with rubber bullets—pushing, shoving, punching—their fellow citizens and members of the press?

Have they abandoned their souls in servitude to leaders devoid of all morals? We know police are capable of better, and we know many of them mean no harm. We understand they're scared, and that daily they take risks the rest of us will never know. We want to see them as our heroes, as exemplary citizens, but they've let us down.

We ask them to search their souls, and that of their fellow officers and their precinct, and reconsider their role and vow to change ways from within. We need them to be the shield we hired them to be, not the source of further suffering.

It is never too late to stand up for one's country and put aside unhealthy alliances with those who seek to oppress the People and subvert the legal system. For it is those who oppress who will also put them so callously on the front lines, to face the scorn and wrath of their brothers and sisters.

We ask them to vote with their feet and their badge, leave the service if they find it cuts against their conscience, speak out and say their peace — invoke their conscience somehow.

We ask them to lay down their weapons and overhaul their systems. We urge them to think of their own children when they wind up to strike with a baton, for that is another man's child. We urge them to think of their own grandfather when they push an elder to the ground.

Certainly, the pain and suffering is not lost upon them, for in their past they must know that feeling of bullying or overbearance.

Certainly, they're big enough to see these acts for the barbarism that they are and to understand that it has no place in our day and age, and that they themselves need not commit atrocities to feel good about themselves and be complete.

Those are the ways of the past, but this is not the future of America. Say it isn't so. These are the errors of the past, but this is not the future of America. Say it isn't so. These are the horrors of the past, but this is not the future of America. Say it isn't so.

We urge them to take the lead and help to mend this Nation, rekindling their resolve and those of their peers, to truly be of service to the Republic and to restore law and order to its proper place.

When they have done that, they will have performed one of the greatest services possible and will have regained the eternal respect and gratitude of their Country.

Can they separate the wheat from the chaff and get their house in order?

The Unruly Rule of Law

With regard to law and order on a larger scale, what has become of the rule of law, for it now seems neither lawful nor orderly.

And what is this "rule of law" anyway, and to where has it fled so swiftly?

If this elusive rule of law is little more than a hopeful but weak aim at equality, then we've fallen terribly short of the mark.

How can something so central to our core of lawful being, to our constitution as a nation of laws, suddenly reveal itself to be so unsure and unsettled?

How can a nation conceived by lawyers not have ironclad protocols and safeguards that protect the tenderness of the Republic? Wasn't a lawful and orderly Republic a chief concern of our founders?

Have we come all these 250 years only to discover we are governed by little more than Gentlemen's Agreements?

Where are the teeth to our laws when we need them, for the things which truly matter, like the protection of our democratic freedoms? Out on the street, the law comes down with great force, but in the squeaky clean halls of government, or on Wall Street, there are only the lightest of reproaches, as if not to upset those who would abuse their significant powers.

How is it that we, the citizens, must wake to find there are, in actuality, few real protections for us?

Politicians kowtow and grovel for the keys to re-election, losing sight of their most profound task to support and defend the Constitution — to first provide service to country rather than putting their interests above the law.

Gone are the watchdogs to clamp down on those in government who foster abuse and nurture corruption. Why are the independent councils and Congressional investigations not better protected from being undermined by the very people whom they are inspecting, such as the Justice Department and the State Department? Why are the protections of whistleblowers not more sacrosanct?

How is it that members of the Executive branch are allowed to bully, intimidate and threaten witnesses? Where are all the checks and balances against the power of those in authority? Where are the lines that should never be crossed and the sacred laws that prevent offenders from crossing treasonous boundaries, such as allowing the interference of foreign powers into our elections, without grave penalties?

The protections are there for those in power who stand to do the greatest damage, but less so for the powerless who choose to speak out against injustice. Why is there such widespread immunity for misconduct? It is those of the highest positions in government who should warrant the greatest of scrutiny, not the least.

If a man steals a TV, we are fully prepared to throw the book at him — three strikes and you're out — but if a man steals an entire government, we gently rap him on the knuckles and mutter with exasperation: Boys will be boys.

Executive Power

How can a governmental system, known throughout the world for its checks and balances, allow a single person to reign freely like a despotic monarch?

Our chief Executive retains the power to hire and fire those members of the Justice Department whose job it is to independently check his powers. Were there no takeaways from all the days of the Nixon era that would now make this impossible?

Our chief Executive may, evidently, privately benefit from his position, using that leverage with corporate and foreign powers to do his bidding. Is the Emoluments Clause merely a fantastical figure, no more real than Santa Claus?

How is it that the President wields such powers to enlist private, unaccountable armies with which to combat and subdue the People?

How can one man's supreme lack of compassion, and his inability to act on behalf of the People, be allowed to condemn hundreds of thousands of Americans to death as a result of his malpractice of the highest office? A single man, in perfect ignorance and over the advice of our top health experts, gets the final word on whether certain States who favor him are protected from the pandemic — through testing (or not), receiving their allotment of ventilators (or not), or whatever else is required for sufficient health.

Where is the pushback? Where is the nerve?

Is it not the duty of House and Senate committees — "Congressional oversight" — to rein in the powers of the President? Where have they been? These and others charged with constraining presidential power have, for quite some time, yielded their powers and duties to the Executive. It is indeed within Congress's duty to pass laws that overrule improper agency decisions, or to narrow the scope of departments deemed not to be following their assigned mandates.

And if it is in the powers of Congress to withhold the purse strings of the nation, why do they not leverage their appropriations? For what can happen in the country, or any household, without the dispensation of funding?

Even so, when the President has tried to go around Congress to access funding, via a series of executive actions, why must we be met with repeated questions from the press: "It's unclear whether he has the legal authority to do that." He doesn't — it couldn't be clearer in the Constitution.

How is it that a President can appoint his own officers — like personal lawyers — to do his bidding with foreign governments such as Ukraine, without confirmation from Congress, which is vested with that authority, as granted by the Constitution?

How can a President so abuse the power to pardon, releasing or commuting the sentences of a long string of personal associates — like Roger Stone, Conrad Black and Joe Arpaio — or people accused of war crimes in Iraq and Afghanistan? This power is evidently one of the most unregulated powers given to presidents, but it has never been overreached in quite this way before.

And where is the State Department? How can there be

no better protections in place to mitigate the ability for a bad executive actor to subvert and debilitate vital parts of government like this one?

Are there really no protections in place to keep executive appointees from undermining the agencies they were hired to run, like the Environmental Protection Agency, Education, Labor or Justice?

And what of our Judicial branch? Why does it not possess the power to play a more central role in checking executive power at times like this? They are all about the laws, yet on their watch there is rampant lawlessness.

Is it too much to ask for strict adherence to this so-called rule of law, under penalty of censure, impeachment or removal from office? Since when are the laws of the Republic optional and non-binding? How is it allowed that the executive branch can simply opt to not heed subpoenas by members of Congress?

And what are the job duties of the President, anyway? Perhaps there is clarity in those descriptions.

The President is "commander-in-chief of the armed forces." It is not his job, however, to declare war, which comes from Congress.

The President has the "power to grant reprieves and pardons for offenses against the United States, except in cases of impeachment."

The President, with the Senate's consent, can make treaties.

The President, with the Senate's consent, can make appointments of "ambassadors, other public ministers and consuls, judges of the supreme court, and all other officers." He also receives ambassadors when they visit.

The President periodically gives to Congress a State of the Union address.

The President "shall take care that the laws be faithfully executed."

That's about it. For all that a president does, one of the most significant jobs in the world, this is as poor of a job description that was ever written by a Human Resources manager.

We are now seeing the frailty of indefinite governmental guidelines and the defects of human character play out in this dicey experiment in democracy. We have witnessed a great erosion of ethical guidelines surrounding the executive branch and the privilege it assumes.

Could anything have been done, though, to prevent it? Of course. The Republicans in the 116th Senate were in a position to check the unbridled powers of the Executive branch, but let history show that they did nothing, breaking their larger vows to Constitution and country in favor of pledging their allegiance and fealty to an individual—a violation of their own job duties.

There is the power of the purse, of appropriations. There is the power of the law, which the President is obliged to execute, if only Congress united around it. There is the power of withholding approval for executive appointment of federal officers and judges. There is the power of impeachment, though we know now how that turned out. But what's been done is now done.

It is inevitable that this administration's behavior will elicit a long stream of books and ongoing discussion about executive power. Here we can barely scratch the surface.

May future generations find a way to clarify this central role and, finally, straighten out this executive mess.

The Separation of Environment & State

Regarding these future generations, other protections are in order, now that we see how one individual's wrong can so vastly impact the natural rights of the other 300+ million.

Some things are too precious to all of us to leave to individual chance and the vicissitudes of human foibles, politics and other whims. Four years—even, God forbid, eight years—may feel like an eternity, but there are issues that encompass such greater areas of importance. I speak of the environment itself.

Presidential tenures and agendas will come and go, but our impact on the environment spills out beyond these fleeting moments. It may require a concerted approach to protect it, and us in it.

The environment itself has no other protectors, or attackers, apart from us. So if it is up to us to decide its fate, then how might we create infallible, enforceable measures that protect us from doing irreparable damage to ourselves and our descendants?

Without such protections, we may well eliminate species that could be our salvation, as with combatting disease and pandemics.

These natural resources, whole species as well as our air, water and land, are far too important to leave to arbitrary human mismanagement and outright abuse.

We are acquainted with the separation of church and state. Is it then too revolutionary to follow this precedent and look for ways to instill environmental protections into our Constitution? This would constitute a separation of environment and state.

Likewise, why not consider binding international laws, in perpetuity, that protect our worldly natural assets and do this as an expansion of the natural rights of men and women? Yes, there have been international accords and protocols and the like, but is there nothing more binding?

This was not a concern of our founders — at the time, the environment itself was, fortunately, not the slightest concern. But I believe our founders would see legislation on this as responsive and responsible government. After all, many of these founders were landowners who worked the land (or, more accurately, had it worked for them) and often expressed a passion for nature.

Today we require a sanctity above and beyond even that of separation of church and state, for while we may live without religion we cannot live without clean air or water. Some things are far too important not to rise above the petty politics of the day.

We would be wise to heed the resounding advice of the global consensus of the world's greatest scientists, and then set about to somehow embed that advise into our global guidelines. Let us create the tightest of international laws, with penalties so severe that no power could violate them without the most serious of consequences from the rest of the world's collective powers—an unbreakable law of the land, air and water.

In Transparency We Trust

Where is transparency in government? Without transparency as an overarching goal, there can be little trust in government.

Transparency of the executive and legislative branches is of particular importance, unless of course we believe that some people, elected elites, are above the law.

Companies force employees to sign legal releases that place parameters on their employment, but our highest officials are seemingly not bound by such things. Is it so unthinkable to demand all records, financial and otherwise, as mandatory requirements before being sworn into office for their new job? What justifiable reason is there to withhold such key information from the public for the most significant positions in government?

And with regard to our common defense, from police to the Pentagon, why don't the People have the right to know much more of what transpires in their own government? What harm is there in shining a light upon those whom we have entrusted to govern?

And once in office, should we drop our guard and cease to strictly monitor the activities of these same personnel?

Of our local defense, why shouldn't it be crystal clear how much a local police department spends on weaponry, on specific types of training, or on protests? Why can't we see, on a simple budget form, how much and in what ways legal expenses are doled out for police misconduct? Yes, that information may be technically "out there," but it shouldn't take a journalist filing a freedom of information request to get it.

With regard to our national defense, the same is true. What keeps the public from knowing how much the Pentagon spends on its Army, Navy, Air Force or Marines, and what exactly is that breakdown? Corporations must produce an annual report that's mailed to all shareholders. Why shouldn't our government adopt the same procedure? Why must we go searching for data on how the Pentagon conducts a war and what the running total expense is?

And why is there still censorship of the press when it comes to the military? Without the clear understanding and imagery of a war, the horrors of war will automatically continue. If the military must shield the public from the battles it fights, then we likely have no business being in that fight.

For better or worse, the public has the right to complete, unfiltered knowledge yet also bears the duty to face up to it. The military wishes to avoid another Vietnam, where the people were informed daily and affected by the media—but is that type of censorship sufficient reason to simply keep the population ignorant of the military's ungoverned behavior?

Regardless of the agency or department though, let's know where we stand, that we can make better-informed decisions about what's in our best interests. How much money has been spent, for instance, in the removal of Post Office boxes and the dismantling of sorting equipment, and why, exactly, was this done?

These agencies and departments of government, without anyone to hold them accountable, will never govern themselves. This is simply a principle of power.

We the People are the consumers and electorate, without whom nothing can happen. We are, essentially, a union of the People. But as it is now, we are a union that doesn't really demand much at all of those in power. In fact, that's because we barely recognize ourselves as an entity, let alone one with immense inherent power. That's a rather apathetic Union.

It is part of our civic duty to raise our awareness and demand new laws with regard to transparency in government at all levels. Never forget that it is the duty of the government to be accountable to the People, not the other way around.

Voting: Duty, Means & Threats

It is also the duty of the People, of course, to vote. This is the contribution of the voice: to speak your conscience for the health of our democratic institutions.

Given the historic difficulty of getting the right to vote at all, you'd think people might embark upon this as a sacred task or, at the least, something worthy of showing up for at the polls.

Originally reserved for white male property owners or taxpayers over 21, no more than 6% of the total population was allowed to vote. Voting has gradually widened to include other groups (in this order): non-white men, women, Native Americans, the Chinese, residents of Washington DC and, finally, 18-year-olds.

In the 1800s, we could count on about 75-80% of the voting age population to vote. This was our best century; unfortunately, it's been mostly downhill from there. By the 1900s, the numbers start to slip, with the 1960s being the strongest decade in the modern era, with roughly 60% of the electorate showing up.

Now we average little over half of eligible voters (55%) doing their civic duty during Presidential years. Half somehow find it not significant enough of an event to leave their house and cast a vote, or even vote by mail. With local elections, it's worse, with just 1 in 5 eligible voters casting a ballot.

Should it be so outrageous and revolutionary to live a country where more than 90% of the electorate votes? Australia can do it, so why can't we? Is it too difficult for American ingenuity to conquer? No—certainly we've managed more daunting challenges.

Citizens should be called upon for a higher standard of voting behavior. Is there anything wrong with strongly encouraging people to vote, either through incentives or penalties? If this seems an affront to your sense of right and wrong, then ask yourself if it's any more shocking than allowing things to continue in this presently pathetic condition.

We penalize our citizens for failure to pay taxes. Is the paying of taxes any more fundamental as a civic duty than voting? Those who don't vote are a slap in the face to our founders. Those who don't vote, through their non-participation, contribute to the slow but steady destruction of democracy.

Yet before we are even to vote, we're confronted by a host of fundamental problems with the voting system itself. If a voter lacks faith in the system, is it any wonder that person might not care to vote at all?

A still greater offense is with those who advocate for the suppression of votes. We've seen this in such things as the dismantling of the postal system in order to limit mail-in voting.

We also see how rigged voting systems still are through various obstacles. Since 2010, state legislatures have created hundreds of new laws that make it more difficult to vote.

These include overly restrictive voter ID regulations, such as onerous photo ID requirements — 15 states now have new laws like these on the books.

We've seen the intentional limiting of voting locations, with nearly 1,200 polling places closed across Southern states since a Supreme Court ruling in 2013 weakened landmark voting rights laws. Particularly notorious have been states like Arizona, Texas, Mississippi and Louisiana. In Georgia, seven counties have only one polling place. What is a reasonable amount of time for a person to wait in line to vote? 10 minutes? 30 minutes? 3 hours?

Gerrymandering continues to disenfranchise voters, predominantly aimed at those on the Left, yet the Supreme Court fumbles along and refuses to make a federal decision that would solve this perennial injustice once and for all, for both parties.

There are plenty of attempts to prevent early voting, with 10 states adding such restrictions since 2010.

There are mass purges of voting rolls, with 12 states making it harder to register and stay registered. Again, since 2010, this strategy has been on the rise.

If we truly value fairness in America, then why shouldn't any form of voting suppression be treated as a felony? Again, the possible solutions are often much easier than we imagine. Sweden, for example, automatically registers all citizens to vote by using data from their national population database.

There are voting protections under the Constitution. The 15th Amendment states, "The right of citizens of the United States to vote shall not be denied or abridged by the United States or by any State on account of race, color, or previous condition of servitude." And yet these practices are still allowed in many situations.

But there are those who seem to constantly seek loopholes around such voting laws. It seems that it would've been a more successful amendment if it had simply said: "The right of citizens of the United States to vote shall not be denied or abridged."

Here again, legal ambiguity abounds. Voting protections are rarely if ever invoked.

And yet this is our most basic contribution to the Republic: the belief in the ballot and the sacred power of the vote. Is it not well past time to codify voting protections into law, or to greatly clarify or strengthen existing protections?

A key obstacle to maintaining the 1965 Voting Rights Act has been the Supreme Court. In 2013, SCOTUS gutted the act, requiring Congress to update it, which still hasn't happened as of 2020.

Our voting systems require reformation and monitoring to ensure voting will again be a sacred rite. To better ensure fairness, we must eliminate, once and for all, strategies that inhibit fair voting: gerrymandering, voting roll purges, the closing of poll locations, restrictions on early voting or mail-in voting, etc. Each of these tactics is anti-democratic, regardless of which political party is guilty of it.

And what about a Voting Day? Can we not strike out a holiday, like Columbus Day, in favor of Voting Day? And why always on a Tuesday? As usual, we make things so much more difficult than they need to be. Can we not displace the day to a weekend in order to maximize turnout, as they do in Brazil?

Apart from the experience of voting itself, what to make of the means and structure of voting? For instance, is it any wonder that voters lack faith in a system that involves the Electoral College, where one vote doesn't mean one vote? Instead we have a convoluted system, like the Senate itself, designed to discourage true democracy.

If the Electoral College were there to protect us from rogue elements getting into our hallowed office of the President, then certainly our current situation is evidence that the system is broken and does not serve its original purpose. It fails to support democracy and should therefore be abolished or, at the least, reformed or recreated.

Reformed how? Doesn't that go against the Constitution? Not at all—it's up to us to decide. We can develop whatever system we want. There are plenty of better systems, too, when it comes to selecting candidates.

For instance, "Ranked Choice Voting" is just one of many, but is likely a top option in that it allows for multiple presidential (or other) candidates to all have a fair say. It also doubly helps to tone down the partisan division, as there's more room for each of the candidates to convey their platforms and make their case. It has the extra merit of perhaps being the most realistic and effective update of the electoral college.

But if we cannot update the electoral college, then perhaps it should be entirely abolished and recreated. We might replace it with an existing, proven model such as proportional representation, as we find in many advanced European countries. These systems are used worldwide by most true democracies such as of the Scandinavian countries, and more generally equitable countries like New Zealand.

And is it any wonder that voters lack faith in a system

where only millionaires and billionaires are able to run for elected office?

Campaign finance reform is needed to ensure that a greater advantage isn't given to a candidate simply by the fact that they have greater financial resources from wealthy donors, corporations, special interest groups or that candidate's personal inheritance.

A more balanced approach had been the American way for nearly all of the past 100 years. Then along came the Citizens United case, posing unnecessary threats to our voting system by allowing big money to enter politics. It's one of the worst, and most unpopular, decisions ever made by the Supreme Court.

Let us return a measure of normalcy to campaign finance regulation. Even if the Supreme Court can't see the light, most Americans are able to see the risks to a system permanently ruled by dark money special interests and super PACs.

But barring a reversal of Citizens United, what else could we do to take these large amounts of money out of politics?

As usual, we've taken something that needn't be difficult and have instead made a huge, dramatic mess out of it. We could create new legislation that gives each candidate the same flat amount of funding that's essentially public financing for their campaigns, and no more. It sounds radical, but why not? Do not confuse free speech with an infinite amount of speech. Candidates in other countries don't have to amass a war chest of $100 million to run a successful campaign to determine a country's next leader. Norway, for instance, does something like this quite successfully, leaving them a lot of money to put to better use.

Meanwhile, back in the U.S., "congressional candidates collected and disbursed $1.6 billion [and] political action committees (PACs) raised and spent $4 billion in the 24-month [campaign] period."

Aren't there better uses in America for all this money? Germany's parties, by contrast, release just one 90-second ad.

And the waste of time, too, is staggering. No election campaign in Canada, for example, has gone on longer than ten weeks. In the U.S., we take about two years for a presidential campaign.

But if we absolutely insist on not taking the easy route, then changes like the ones I've indicated may need to be regulated at all levels of elections: local, state and national. We can do this the hard way or the easy way.

Higher & Higher Education

Education is intertwined with voting. It is the duty of the People to educate themselves, so as to be an informed electorate — this is contribution of the mind.

Regarding the duty of the People to educate themselves that we may have an informed electorate, wouldn't we be remiss if we failed to offer our People the most ample means to that proper education?

For what better tool is there to ensure that the People are always in pursuit of Happiness than to provide them with this key to meaningful lives and personal enlightenment?

The founders were, mostly, a highly educated group, so they are, in terms of their educational levels of study, great examples to model. It was a preeminent concern of theirs that an ignorant, low-class populace could not be entirely trusted, and that systems needed to be put into place to prevent the influence of a meddling and troublesome Democracy.

Then why not help to raise up these masses of people? It's a fitting solution to educate our electorate by any means necessary. Why couldn't a proper college education, for instance, be the birthright and obligation of all Americans? If that were the case, then there would be no further need to pit ourselves against ourselves, as our founders did — to brace the door against Democracy herself.

Having a truly informed population should, at least logically, remove the argument of mistrust of the People to assist in shaping government. If the People were worthy in the eyes of our founders in this respect, then the People's participation in government would no longer be a just reason for concern.

Why wouldn't we want to redouble our efforts to better educate our People, to create a broad program of studies, from birth through college, that's free for all Americans?

Education is a fundamental key to success in America. Why wouldn't we want to make every effort toward substantially expanding in this area? No American should be without the opportunity to expand their knowledge and be more competitive in the global workplace. An educated America is a strong America.

If only we could do this, we'd have less need to search abroad for the right workers; we'd have more homegrown workers who possess substantial and desirable skills.

And if we were serious about getting all our citizens up to speed with their higher education, then wouldn't we also want that education to start as early as possible? Wouldn't we want our youngest Americans to have the greatest advantages, a head start, in the right direction? Free preschool education would go a long way toward completing a top-to-bottom educational system for all citizens.

An educated citizenry is one of the best ways to ensure an informed, robust system of self-government while also solidifying our workforce. What are we waiting for?

At Your Service

And what of the duty of the People to provide civil service to country? It is the duty of the People to give back to the country — this is the contribution of body and spirit.

It has been many years since sacrifice through national service was mandatory. Conscription was formerly only for men, and then only to go to war — ending, as it did, after the Vietnam War. Since then our military has been limited to a relatively small group of participants, creating a wide gap between those who serve their country in this way and those who don't.

In being a service member, one is thrown into contact with a cross section of Americans from all walks of life. In this time of great partisan division, wouldn't a program like this represent a timely new system of national healing?

Why not once again seek the participation of our young adults, to dedicate a year or two of service to their Nation, except with a widening scope of services offered? This is how it is in Israel — simply a part of coming of age and duty to country.

Why not build a healthy sense of agency and joint ownership in the Nation and its various domestic and worldly activities? The spirit of service has, at times, been a powerful force in our culture, but we seem to have gone too long without it. John F. Kennedy's inspiring words in the 1960s (..."ask not what your country can do for you"...) led to an unprecedented surge in civic pride and service.

To serve a cause larger than oneself, whether voluntary or mandatory, is a noble mission that can yield a valuable perspective to participants and valuable labor for the country. A program such as this — a national service initiative — could constitute an inspiring venture for America's young men and women, and additionally give rise to training and skills for career advancement beyond the period of service.

And yet it's not fair nor necessary that all such service members would be expected to only serve in defense capacities. Fortunately, there is an equal need for many other types of service to be performed via peaceable means.

A National Service Corps would populate the ranks of our existing branches and extend to other areas, too. There would be the option for regular enlistment for a period of time on the federal level in: the Army, the Navy, the Air and Space Force, or the Marine Corps. There could also be the option to fulfill our needs for domestic defense, on the state level, by fulfilling our 2nd Amendment duties. To support the intent of our founders to have "a well regulated Militia," participants could opt to serve in their state's National Guard.

Let us, likewise, supply ample options to serve to some extent in the Coast Guard, AmeriCorps or the Peace Corps, and provide comparable programs dedicated to, say, science, technology and the environment.

Let us create WPA-like work programs (as in the 1930s) intended to keep America's infrastructure of roads, rails and bridges intact, and add air travel and homeland security services to its jurisdiction.

In short, we're failing to use a huge pool of human resources for the steady improvement of our country.

By interweaving the population in this manner we can create a positive and unified patriotic spirit that fosters goodwill among all citizens, thus contributing to a Happiness and Tranquility among the People.

Taxation, Debts & Welfare

What progress can be made of taxation, that favorite topic which extends back to our founding years and our fundamental grievance with England? It was that which, at least in part, compelled us to separation.

Taxation is that enemy which all people can rally against, as we all agree on its disagreeability.

Certainly most Americans would not argue if the forms for taxation should be vastly reformed and simplified, and that there should be greater equity in payment by all citizens.

For individuals, what if no taxpayer form could be longer than a few pages? After all, the first income tax form was just a single page. How much stronger might our balance sheet be if we could eliminate all loopholes? Again, who among the 99% would take issue with these reforms?

Or, consider countries like New Zealand and Japan, where the government sends you what they believe you owe, then you either accept or reject their calculations. It takes anywhere from 1-5 minutes to "complete" individual taxes each year. Americans seem to enjoy much longer dramas.

Not so long ago, companies paid taxes based on tax rates that Congress dictated — just as we individual citizens did. After WWII, in 1947, federal revenue was evenly derived from individuals and corporations at roughly 40% each. Taken together, this mostly funded the government. The effective corporate tax rate was set at about 50%.

The idea of companies not paying anything was unheard of, unthinkable. Today, however, it's commonplace to hear of enormously profitable companies not paying any taxes whatsoever.

Between 2008-2012, 111 profitable Fortune 500 firms paid $0 in federal taxes in at least one of those five years. By 2018, that trend continued and now seems to include refunds: Duke Energy earned $11 billion in U.S. income and got a refund for $647 million. Amazon also reported $11 billion income but received a federal income tax rebate of $129 million. IBM made just $500 million yet received a federal income tax rebate of $342 million. Netflix paid $0 in federal income tax on $856 million of U.S. income.

To most hard-working taxpayers, all this seems genuinely outrageous. Is it too much to ask that everyone pitch in, including corporations? Since when did paying taxes become nearly optional?

Today, while individual Americans foot the largest portion of the federal bill every year, 48%, corporate America picks up just 9% of the tab. This is because, since 1947, the effective corporate tax rate dropped by more than half, to 21%. So, in dollar amounts, the corporate share of federal tax revenue fell by nearly two-thirds over 60 years—from 32% in 1952 to 10% in 2013. And this is despite the fact that, starting in the late '80s, corporate profits began to skyrocket while wages for regular Americans generally flattened or even declined.

Maybe, in another decade or so, American workers will allow all Fortune 500 companies to avoid paying any taxes. Individuals will simply absorb the remaining 9% now paid by corporations and the People will be expected to pay 60% or maybe even 70% of the costs of running our government.

If we don't stick up for our interests better, then you can be sure that corporations will naturally do whatever they can do to pay the absolute least amount possible. It's simply in their nature.

Was Congress established to serve corporations or the People? How can we reverse these trends that fail to promote the general welfare and, instead, only serve to further advance the corporate welfare system?

How can we right the wrongs that give privilege to the few while taking taxes from the many? How can we regain the more than $1.3 trillion in lost revenue caused by such loopholes—that's 6.3% of our GDP, more than outlays for Social Security or Medicare and Medicaid combined.

What can we, as a country, do to reestablish justice and enshrine into law that corporations must pay their fair share—at a minimum, equal to or greater than the huge burden put upon the average American family?

And regarding loopholes, why not close them all, including tax-evasion tactics like offshore tax havens?

What is a reasonable minimal percentage for corporations to pay? Why not stipulate an effective tax rate on their gross income with a minimum amount? No exceptions, no loopholes.

Must we make this aspect of our common finances also more complicated than it needs to be?

Let us explore new ways for government to be funded in lieu of taxes, like public-private partnerships that share profits with the government, along the lines of what we did with General Motors during the Great Recession. If this happened on a large enough scale, perhaps it might be possible to abolish taxes altogether, or at least limit them substantially.

As our founders were truly perplexed with the problem of how to pay off their $72 million in debts, we likewise have reason to be concerned.

In 2019, our national debt stood at roughly $25,000,000,000,000—as in, $25 trillion, give or take a penny.

That debt now exceeds the size of our entire economy. It has never been as high as it is now (except just after WWII), as measured by the percentage of our gross domestic product. As with a household mortgage, a certain measure of debt is acceptable to expand one's assets and do great things in the world with capital. But what level of debt is deemed sustainable? A consensus standard of debt is not to exceed 60% of government debt-to-GDP. Currently, in the era of Covid-19, the U.S. debt has risen sharply to about 100%.

And what of our trade deficit with other countries? Ours is the largest in the world, at $627,700,000,000 — as in $627 billion — which is a rate at least four times as large as most other developed countries. These deficits are generally measured in terms of the current account balance (CAB) of a country. The U.S. deficit is four times larger than the next highest country, the U.K. The recommended CAB standard is not to exceed -100,000 (in million US dollars). How long can we sustain our levels of deficit imbalance before it becomes a long-term fiscal disability?

And what of our budget? Is it so wrong to demand that it be balanced? Many states have such a balanced budget requirement, but this practice doesn't exist on the federal level. Such a law was never part of our Constitution, though unsuccessful attempts have been made for a balanced budget amendment. At least nine countries "have constitutional rules about budget balance or deficits." Why should the federal government be exempt from this practice?

The time has come for America to enact bold fiscal legislation that sets strict limits on our spending, so we can avert a major future crisis.

The Failure of Parties & Their Representatives

Regardless of party affiliation, most Americans would probably agree that both of our political parties are deeply flawed, each in their own way.

Democrats, out of desperation, fear and a lack of vision and guts, generally fight to put forward only the most blandest and middling of candidates, casting a wide net with those believed to be the best defense against the far-right, undermining all other voices across the liberal spectrum. Progressives are shut out as a threat to business as usual.

Republicans, having drunk the Kool-Aid of the Mad King, have entered a death spiral of corruption and moral failure. Having swept into office with the notion to drain the swamp, they've only made it far worse. True conservatives are forced to quit the party or abandon their principles and fall in line with a platform that mostly betrays their traditional values.

And, of course, money in politics increasingly rules both parties in ways that primarily support corporations and only secondarily support the people and democracy.

The system has evolved to the point where it's not open to change, and this political paralysis is detrimental to the nation's evolution. Its encouragement of division and rancor constitutes a very real threat to the health of the nation. The prospect of dueling political parties was one of the chief nightmares of our founders, especially for Washington, Madison and Hamilton — though less so for people like Jefferson.

It's in our history to have more than just Democratic and Republican parties; it's just that the stories of those other parties are usually fleeting and unsuccessful. Since 1854, with the disbanding of the Whig party, our two major parties have been firmly established.

In fact, it's been argued that we don't in fact have "broken" political parties at all. Rather, for the last 160 years they've been doing what parties do: consolidating power while eliminating competition. If these were the two sole businesses in an industry, we would likely seek to break up their uncompetitive control of the market.

Authors at the Harvard Business Review note that a "polit-ical-industrial complex" developed over time that has been "perversely optimized — or even expressly created — by and for the benefit of the entrenched duopoly at the center of our political system."

The authors go on to conclude that, essentially, though we

like to think of our political parties as having "high-minded principles and impartial structures and practices derived from the Constitution," they are not—they are like competitive businesses in any other industry, seeking to limit entry to new competition. Furthermore, since there are no significant forces that can compete with this system, it naturally perpetuates itself. And finally, they note that "business, in pursuing its short-term interests, has become a major participant in the political-industrial complex, exacerbating its dysfunction. The business community must reexamine its engagement model and throw its weight behind structural political innovation that would benefit both business and society in the long term."

If we want to break this hold and gain more choice in our political system, how are we to achieve that? With many other attempts having failed, it seems inevitable that something unconventional and untried must be attempted: Might we more boldly expand our party system to include, say, a minimum of four political parties? If not done decisively at once, however, one party always gains the unfair advantage; if done all at once, perhaps it would be more like a complete reset that provides a chance to get it right.

For example, why couldn't one of the parties be a truly conservative Republican Party, in the traditional sense—a more moderate faction? And how about a more radical faction on the Right, likely a Libertarian party, which better addresses their particular concerns? Likewise, there would be the traditional Democratic Party—again, a more moderate faction. And then a more radical faction on the Left, likely a Progressive party? Such a party could better speak to the unique concerns of that constituency. And lastly, we've already got an Independent party that allows for all those who don't easily align with any other group.

If we truly believe that the spectrum of our political opinions is underrepresented and that our ideal choices are more nuanced than is currently supported by the tired two-party system, then we need to increase our party system to be more diverse. But a radical shift like this would require concerted Congressional action and a Constitutional amendment, and with a duopoly in power that would mean they'd need to vote against its own interests. For this to work, the People would need to demand unequivocally, and with unity.

Another option, perhaps more realistic, is becoming a popular standard in some states. Ranked Choice Voting (a.k.a. Instant Run-off voting, or Final-Five voting) is a method that helps to avoid choosing between the lesser of two evils, for fear of "splitting your vote." This would create non-partisan ballots where you don't just vote for one candidate – you rank your top five choices. When any one candidate gets over 50% of the vote (after a series of eliminations and recalculations), they are the winner. Voters under this system report being more satisfied with the new process than with our current system. Also, the winner is the person with the broadest appeal; as it is now, we end up with a leader who doesn't even have the support of the majority of the population. Under ranked choice voting, people don't just vote for one of two parties, they vote according to issues they care about most.

Is it any wonder that our political parties have such vastly unpopular reviews when so many of our representatives have long overstayed their welcome and have turned their tenure into life-long professions? This bodes ill for the Republic.

House of Representatives members are no sooner into office than they must jump to the task of re-election every other year. Rather, instead of a mere two years at a time, why not give them somewhat longer terms, but restrict the number of terms that they can ultimately serve?

Senators, with six-year terms, generally seem to have too much time to dig in their heels. What if we gave them the chance for two shorter terms – and maybe no more than a decade or so total?

Justices, like Presidents, do not need life terms. Fifteen years feels like enough time to make one's mark before relinquishing the seat to a younger, eager judge, to give them a chance.

Age limits also need a change. After a certain age, the

freshness of mind, so valuable to the competent functioning of complex law and government, begins to wear.

No President, Senator, member of Congress or Justice should serve longer than, say, the regular retirement age, or thereabouts.

Without a few more checks and balances made on their way into office, we'll surely never get any of them out of office.

Little Brother: The House

Our House of Representatives is the raucous little brother who always gets overridden by his older, trickster sibling.

Bills begin here and eventually get sent on to the Senate, where they most often die—at least under this current administration and the Senate's leadership.

Nearly nothing can be accomplished without the consent of the Senate, for the upper chamber always has the final say. The House may do the legwork to prepare legislation, but they must always go to the Senate, cap in hand. It is then accepted or rejected, with an emphasis on the latter.

In and of itself, what can the House do that has a definitive effect on its own? Not much, it seems. Here is the basic job description for Congress, so we can see more clearly what falls under its jurisdiction:

The House of Representatives "shall have the sole power of impeachment" but the Senate "shall have the sole power to try all impeachments."

Both the House and the Senate can make and pass bills. For instance: "All bills for raising revenue shall originate in the House of Representatives; but the Senate may propose or concur with amendments as on other bills."

Following this, there are roughly twenty or so more duties enumerated in the Constitution. For the sake of brevity, they include the power to: "lay and collect taxes," "pay the debts," "provide for the common defense," provide for the general welfare," "borrow money," "regulate commerce," "establish a uniform rule of naturalization, and uniform laws on the subject of bankruptcies," "coin money," "provide for the punishment of counterfeiting," "establish post offices and post roads," "promote the progress of science and useful arts," "constitute tribunals inferior to the supreme court," "punish pirates," "declare war," "raise and support armies," "provide and maintain a navy," "make rules for the government and regulation of the land and naval forces," "provide for calling forth the militia," "exercise exclusive legislation in all cases whatsoever, over such district [...] as may [...] become the seat of the government of the United States."

These duties, though more specific and plentiful than those of the executive, often pertain to issues that were pertinent to colonial times (i.e., create a navy and post offices, punish counterfeiters and pirates, establish a seat of government, etc.) but are not so relevant to today's world.

Must we be chained to job descriptions that are 250 years old? Isn't it about time we refreshed the duties of Congress, at least to some degree?

Big Brother: The Senate

Meanwhile, the Senate is so poorly conceived that it warrants complete restructuring or outright abolishment. That may sound extreme, but it's been deeply flawed ever since its original, pressured rush to inception in order to appease the smaller states and keep them from walking out of the constitutional convention back in 1787.

Let's take a step back to remember how the Senate evolved the way it did:

The Senate was established as, "a house of elites that would temper the less disciplined people's house" and has been likened to a saucer that cools the hotheaded teacup of the House of Representatives. That is, the Senate was granted the veto power to significantly check the power of the People (i.e., the House of Representatives). Those checks and balances were, and still are, about checks on Democracy herself.

George Rolland Wolfe

Our original governing structure, the Articles of Confederation, was feared to be operating in ways that were too loose knit, too democratic. The upper class framers of the Constitution (which was most of them) sought to "fix" the Articles by pushing for a convention at which to update the government—a U.S. 2.0, of sorts.

After much ado, in 1787 in Philadelphia, they succeeded in changing the government guidelines so that the Constitution would be structured with that anti-democratic bias. Less democracy meant, they hoped, more stability for the markets, for capital.

And so we have our current merger of capitalism and a Republic, assuming we can keep it together.

On the world stage today though, by contrast, most governments have something akin to proportional representation, like in the House because... well, it's more fair and democratic.

The great irony is that we were on the cutting edge of creating a supposedly democratic system of self-government, but now we lag behind nearly all true democracies in the world in this regard.

Our archaic version of the Senate wouldn't even be considered legal if evaluated by the standards of individual states. That's because state legislative districts are required by law to have roughly equal populations. But the U.S. Senate runs contrary to this legal precedent. The Equal Protection Clause of the 14th Amendment demands that there must be a system of "one man, one vote." That means an institution like the US Senate, with wildly unequal populations in its various states (600,000 constituents for some Senators, 40,000,000 for other Senators) should not, either legally or in good conscience, exist.

Fifty percent of our population lives in just nine states, but those nine states are represented by 18 senators; meanwhile, the other fifty percent of our population, get 82 senators.

Given that the growing disparity of power has gone to

citizens from small states (and their Senate representatives) at the expense of the democratic rights of citizens of large states (and their Senators), the time has come to switch to more of a proportional representation system in order to cease violating our own Constitution.

A Wyoming voter now has roughly 66 times as much voting power as a California voter, plus the ability to bring a disproportionate amount of money to their state because of this. With an absurd imbalance like this — far removed from one man, one vote — at what point do we take drastic measures toward realignment?

How about something like this: If your state has up to 2 million citizens, then you get 2 Senators (for at least 30 states, they would still keep their current number of Senators). For each additional 2 million citizens, however, you'd be entitled to receive 2 more Senators (so the largest states, California and Texas, might receive 20 and 15 Senators respectively).

Alternatively, we could solve this by unifying the two chambers under a single roof of Congress (as Nebraska does) with combined job responsibilities. Then we'd simply adopt the system of proportional representation, as the House already does. In that case, there would be a monumental shift toward fair representation, toward true Democracy.

If this intrinsic unfairness in our current system were not enough just in the Senate alone, then consider how it spills over and affects the Executive branch, too.

The Senate model also imbalances the Electoral College, for if California had its rightful number of Senators in reasonable proportion to its population, then it should be entitled to more Electors in each state for Presidential voting. That is, if we used a unicameral system of a single Congress, California would receive its current allotment of 53 members (from the House), but would also gain an extra 20 members (from the Senate), for a total of 73 Electoral votes; Wyoming would receive their current minimum of 2 senators, and would gain 1 House member, for a total of 3 representatives.

You can appreciate how out of kilter and fragile the current system is when the majority of voters consistently wins the popular vote while losing the election.

What we see in the Senate is something new that the founders did not imagine: a Tyranny of the Minority. In short, it's a rigged system. If the representatives and their constituents in these less-populated states acted in ways that were more in sync with the national population, this would not be a problem. But when their beliefs and behaviors become so extreme, then our founders' system fails to provide adequate balance.

Gun control is perhaps a good example: roughly 7 out of 10 Americans are genuinely disturbed by and afraid of the uptick in gun violence, and they support reasonable gun regulation. Attempts by the House to legislate that into being, however, are constantly denied, as the Senate's leaders are unduly influenced by the NRA. These alliances belie the wishes of the larger population.

The 116th Senate has concerned itself only with winning, not in serving, and has subverted a system based on trust, for their personal gain. They have turned what was once term the world's greatest deliberative body into a farce, barely recognizable as a respectable institution in the eyes of Americans and our allies abroad. They have forgotten the advice that "patriotism means to stand by the country. It does not mean to stand by the President."

Here Comes the Judge

At first, the Judiciary would seem to be a last bastion of hope and principled, unbiased judgment, far removed from the influences and mania of the rest of D.C.

Americans cling to the story that our Judiciary issues decisions of great societal impact, putting to rest forever ill-conceived rulings while swooping in to save the day, sticking up for Liberty wherever She is abused. But the Judiciary is not composed of neutral judges who can review laws and issue impartial decisions. Under this administration especially, and under the larger reign of the "Roberts' court," the SCOTUS has turned from being a predominantly even-handed body to one that is primarily and predictably partisan, leaning increasingly to the right now as it adds appointments whose main duty is to serve the interests and do the bidding of the executive, with just a few swing decisions to mix it up a bit.

People are on the verge of losing faith in the Supreme Court, in the Justice Department, and all the way down the chain of courts, including the criminal justice system.

The Supreme Court appears just and lofty until one looks back, with the advantage of hindsight, at many of the decisions that did damage to the country and continue to have a negative effect as current laws:

Dred Scott, just before the Civil War, was the beginning, a warm-up, of sorts: Let's declare that blacks should not be considered American citizens, and bar any laws that might free slaves ;

In a near unanimous ruling that's still in effect, we continue to authorize the forced sterilization of people with intellectual disabilities "for the protection and health of the state" ;

Another nearly unanimous ruling retracted most of the civil rights protections won in the 1870s, clearing the way for racial discrimination in businesses and public accommodations for the next 70+ years ;

The Court's famous "separate but equal" ruling in the 1890s, Plessy v. Ferguson, upheld state segregation laws, ensuring that the gains of the post-Civil War reconstruction era were quickly replaced by decades of Jim Crow laws ;

Child labor in mines and factories? The Court ruled it unfair that Congress would have the gall to ban child labor ;

SCOTUS endorsed the forced relocation of Japanese Americans during WWII, stripping them of their rights as citizens because of the suspicion that they might not be fully loyal — a belief we didn't follow through on for Germans, Italians, or any other groups in the Axis powers ;

As late as 1986, the Court was still criminalizing the sexual activities of those in gay and lesbian relationships ;

And in the 21st century, who could forget Gore v Bush, even regretted later by some justices who voted for it? Why get all the information needed to determine a Presidential election when you could halt the recount of contested ballots and call it a day? Had this trivial decision not been so hastily made, we might've avoided the Iraq War, the war in Afghanistan, the Citizens United ruling, and the Great Recession ;

After the Exxon Valdez oil spill of 1989, one of the worst environmental disasters ever, and after two decades of litigation, Exxon was finally held responsible for its negligent captain running aground and fined $5 billion for damages. But the Roberts Court swooped in and ruled that Exxon couldn't be subject of punitive damages beyond compensatory ones, dropping total damages down to a mere $500 million (a veritable 90%-off sale). Not only did Exxon walk away virtually free of penalties, but the Supreme Court's ruling ended up increasing Exxon's stock value by $23 billion in two days due to the light verdict ;

Perhaps the most hated decision on all sides from the Roberts Court is Citizens United, from 2012. It held that corporations are people and that political donations are essentially speech protected by the First Amendment, opening the floodgates to unlimited personal and corporate donations to super PACs. Though hugely unpopular on all sides, we're stuck with the ruling for a while — it would take a constitutional amendment or a new Supreme Court makeup to reverse the decision .

Some would say all this is sour grapes. Yes, this is true in that it should remind us of the lasting effects that some legal rulings leave upon our country for decades, even centuries.

As with many things in America, the solutions themselves are easy to implement — it's the changing of minds and traditions that's the real problem.

In this case we're trying to solve for the biased appointment of justices by political parties and the growing lack of trust in the courts caused by increasingly partisan politics.

As Americans, we think there's only one method for choosing judicial appointments, but of course there are always many other options, most of them more successful than we use today. We need only look.

After all, these are meant to be lifetime appointments, at least as we have it now. So for something that important, shouldn't we have a more methodical, stringent system that selects these sacred roles of our judiciary in a better way?

For instance, why not increase the number of justices? As our founders knew, there is less chance for wrongdoing when key decisions are shared by the many rather than the few.

We could also select judges based on a merit system of peer evaluation, as determined by the collective opinions of numerous reputable groups, such as the American Bar Association, top Left/Right think tanks, and the recommendations of both houses of Congress, as well as the President. Instead, we insist on one person making the decision and hoping that the Senate will rubberstamp that person through the confirmation process, even if they're far from being the most qualified person for the job.

When other countries select justices to their highest courts, they don't need to brace themselves for great angst and public controversy, as is certainly the case, for instance, in deciding a replacement for Ruth Bader Ginsburg. Instead, politics is taken out of the equation by having a larger number of justices and by using a merit-based system of nomination. The stakes are lower, too, as each decision isn't a do-or-die, lifetime affair.

"Watching the U.S. process is almost like watching a warning sign: 'This is what not to do,'" remarked Emmett Macfarlane, a political scientist at the University of Waterloo in Canada."

There is hope for a much better Judiciary, through vetted methods such as the ones mentioned above, but it won't find peace without bold change through the will of the people and their representatives.

The State of our Military

We have built our military to be a powerhouse, and it certainly is. It's managed by capable generals and serviced by loyal soldiers of all ranks. Led correctly, arguably, it can even be a force for peace, through deterrence.

The military's budget is a sacred cow that no politician seems willing or able to budge, for who wants to say we need less protection? There can never be enough national defense, right? Just like there can never be enough police on the streets, right? Is there a price tag that's simply too much to spend on our national defense?

It can safely be reasoned that U.S. military expenditures, being roughly the size of the next seven largest military budgets combined, have gone overboard. And this is in light of the fact that, of the top 15 militaries in the world, 12 of them are our allies. And while it's true that countries like Saudi Arabia and Russia spend a larger % of their GDP on military, they pale by comparison in total expense.

We spend 54% of our discretionary budget on the military — that is, funds that come from taxes.

Our basic total military spending is approximately $600-700 billion, with China, in second, with $260 billion, followed by India with $70 billion and Russia with $65 billion. And so on.

Roughly one-sixth of our federal spending goes to national defense. And even that leaves out a lot that falls under other aspects of Defense, such as the Department of Defense (DoD), the Veterans Administration (VA), the National Nuclear Security Administration (NNSA), and portions of the Intelligence Community's (IC) non-military intelligence program — for a gross total of approximately $950 billion, not even including programs like the Department of Homeland Security ($70 billion) or the FBI ($10 billion).

So, rounding off: roughly $1 trillion.

After a certain point, with all the zeroes, our minds go numb: a single Tomahawk missile runs us $1.4 million; a fighter jet costs us a cool $14-18 million per; a destroyer-class ship goes for somewhere between $1.8-$4.2 billion (we currently have about 70 of these); and so on.

This is truly Big Government. It is Military Welfare. It is a huge culture tied to our defense and, if necessary, to war.

Perhaps part of our problem is that of the imagination — that is, we can't envision how we might better use that money, so it's easier to just keep the status quo in place and funnel money into this giant budget-buster.

And yet, if the budget were cut and there was another terrorist attack on America, it would be an uncomfortable stance to have taken. Still, we must be prepared to make the hard decisions, not just the most popular. Parents don't allow kids to eat endless amounts of candy, or carry around live weapons — it doesn't make the parent bad, it makes them into a responsible parent.

We must likewise be savvy stewards of our budget, and of concerns for future generations. To allow for virtually unlimited funds to go to the military is unfeasible, given our current debts, deficits and in consideration of the general welfare of the People, who are sacrificed in the process.

President Eisenhower said, "As we peer into society's future, we — you and I, and our government — must avoid the impulse to live only for today, plundering for our own ease and convenience the precious resources of tomorrow. We cannot mortgage the material assets of our grandchildren without risking the loss also of their political and spiritual heritage. We want democracy to survive for all generations to come, not to become the insolvent phantom of tomorrow."

Yes, we care about having a substantial Defense. But we also need to spread our funds around in ways that more daily affect the lives of civilian Americans, too. A portion of funding could, for example, go a long way toward programs that promote economic security and shared prosperity for all Americans. Consider that we lose 150,000 Americans every year to "deaths of despair" (i.e., groups whose social and economic outlook is bleak and who are therefore prone to suicide, alcoholic liver disease, and drug overdose). That's about 2 ½ times the total number of Americans killed during the entire Vietnam War.

The military's ties to corporate interests takes away from the societal need to care for our people and instead places those funds in the hands of those primarily serving their company's interests.

Regarding the military's connection with corporate America, Eisenhower warned as he left office: "...we must guard against the acquisition of unwarranted influence, whether sought or unsought, by the military-industrial complex. The potential for the disastrous rise of misplaced power exists and will persist. We must never let the weight of this combination endanger our liberties or democratic processes. We should take nothing for granted. Only an alert and knowledgeable citizenry can compel the proper meshing of the huge industrial and military machinery of defense with our peaceful methods and goals, so that security and liberty may prosper together."

Let's assume for a moment that we were able to have a robust military that still dwarfed each of the next five top militaries in the world. If we cut even 5%, we would barely feel the difference. What else might we be able to afford our people if we reevaluated spending in this way?

If we look at our complete expenditure of about $1 trillion/year, and if we were able to trim 10%, we'd still be left with $900 billion for the military, more than three times that of China and fifteen times as much as Russia. But that would allow us to make free college tuition a reality at public universities for all Americans, at an estimated cost of $75 billion. With the remaining $25 billion, we might also be able to make fixes to our public rail system (Amtrak) , our postal system , and make a sizable and significant first payments toward lowering our national debt.

If we were able to trim 20%, we'd be left with $800 billion for the military, still many more times that of China and twelve times as much as Russia. What might that allow us to do? We could, additionally, fund free pre-K education for all American families. We could provide very generous incentives, like in the G.I. Bill did after WWII, to make it much easier for all Americans to participate in home and land ownership plus gain access to Wall Street's benefits, creating capital and portfolios that they could build upon to be more secure in their own finances. Plus, this would help drive the economy. We could kick-start a private-public revolution of green energy as part of our legacy, reducing our fossil fuel emissions by a robust 40% while creating an estimated 3 million new jobs.

If we could trim 30%, we'd still have $700 billion for the military, nearly three times that of China and ten times Russia. What might that allow us to do? We could begin to implement free Medicare for all Americans, converting the monthly amounts we give up with every paycheck and out of pocket expenses into a bonus refund each month for all households, in perpetuity.

And that's just what we could do by streamlining existing military programs, trimming the fat and forcing greater efficiency into the system, refocusing on whatever areas end up mattering most, after all is said and done.

We must accept that the lives of our civilians are no less valuable than the lives of our soldiers, and that civilians need vital support to survive, too.

Healthy, Stealthy & Wise

How is it that our healthcare system is the only one among major industrialized nations that still doesn't provide healthcare to the majority of its citizens?

Though we have excellent care for some, and we can tout our innovative surgical procedures, healthcare technology, medical education, top doctors, and the like, we have failed miserably at an equitable distribution of care for tens of millions of our citizens.

Can we pivot and better care for our people?

For starters, do you suppose we might all be guaranteed

excellent healthcare, at low or no cost, if it were simply the law that, whatever system is good enough for our President, Senators, House members and Judiciary is good enough for all Americans?

Yes, that ought to lead to actions that would provide all of us with the proper healthcare we need.

Healthcare is far too big of a topic to solve here, but there's no shortage of vetted roadmaps, viable worldwide precedents and other detailed plans to implement.

When the people demand it, by and by, loud and clear, it will happen.

An Immigrant Walks into a Bar

One thing most Americans can agree on is that our immigration system has seen better days — it is, likely, broken.

For a country that in so many ways is defined by immigration — a steady stream of foreigners making the United States their home — it's ironic that again we seem to lag behind other major countries when it comes to a thoughtful, clear and coherent policy.

Of the many different systems to choose from in the world, we've prioritized the "family-based" model. It's one that has a strong emotional element, in that we like the idea of families staying together as a unit. Who doesn't? But is it really the best model to work from? Something about it clearly isn't working.

All in all, when it comes to immigration, we fluctuate between being either too lenient (everyone should be able to come) or too severe (we need walls and scare tactics to keep certain people out). Without clear guidelines and protections, according to principles that transcend the vicissitudes and politics of individual administrations, it's not realistically possible to find workable solutions.

As with healthcare, there are enough systems out there that we need not reinvent the wheel. Rather, let us adopt a model that works best, or nearly best, and conform it to our particular aims and circumstances.

Arguably, Canada offers a worthy base model. It's a merit-based system (i.e., a determination is made on a person's estimated value to the country). Might we adopt some version of these basic criteria, and then adapt them to create an optimal American version?

The danger of the Canadian model, apparently, is in being too restrictive for the needs of an aging population, leaving not enough workforce to fill all needed jobs. In that case, we might consider increasing new immigration to 1.5 million per year from our current average of roughly 750,000. And with those numbers we might doubly reduce the backlog of those seeking a path to citizenship: that of DACA (700,000) and currently undocumented workers (10.7 million, 3% of total population).

Additionally, why not affix a healthy goal for a planned number of foreign-born citizens? At present we are at 14%; perhaps we endow a merit-based system with this extra measure of diversity, at a number such as 18%. This would help to counter what might be construed as a system that's too coldly pragmatic (i.e., based on merit) while still providing the order we so badly need and encouraging the diversity we expect as a country of immigrants.

Additionally, there is also the need to clarify and update our temporary worker system so as to allow for a larger share of temporary workers, to discourage the number of future undocumented workers.

These new goals might seem strange to an American temperament, but they are ultimately in sync with a Nation determined to have both firm laws and a compassionate approach, as befits the essence of our character and history.

Firearms

Americans are actually not divided when it comes to reasonable gun control measures.

As recent years have all too clearly shown, violent crime with unmanaged and undocumented firearms, has unleashed a stream of tragedies that would likely have been preventable.

Like it or not, American gun ownership is part of the American way, and the solution is not likely to be found in banning all guns so much as, like any product, regulating them so that they are as safe as possible in the lives of all consumers and the public at large.

Given the open borders that a state-by-state approach leaves, measures in one state will inevitably face great difficulty in trying to counter the negative effects of those states that don't adhere to the same system of firm laws. Federal action is not only sensible but also necessary toward ensuring the maximum safety and welfare of the People.

Most universally acceptable are mandatory universal background checks that would prohibit purchases by those with issues not compatible with responsible gun use. This would include those not fully in control of their faculties, and those who have shown themselves to be violent.

A "cooling off" period on purchases would also seem to be an additional tactic with little controversy.

As our citizens are required to earn a license before they can drive, it would be entirely sensible for each state to likewise require a gun license or a permit that displays proof of residency in that jurisdiction, each state thus keeping a registry of all firearm sales.

To assure a seamless process, all sales would likely need to be done only through a licensed state dealer, as opposed to the dangers of undocumented guns transferred through gun show loopholes.

Education is a component surrounding any potentially damaging product, from driving vehicles to firing weapons. Proof of completion of thorough firearms training would need to be required for all firearms purchases. We expect no less of people learning to fly a private plane, in order to keep planes from dropping from the sky and dotting the landscape with countless tragedies.

Also in the realm of education would be the need for elimination of all restrictions on funding studies about guns, gun violence, and all other healthcare-related topics related to firearm use that are now prohibited.

And as with any vehicle, mandatory gun insurance, with proof of secure storage for firearms, would be necessary. Should owners of firearms be less accountable and legally liable due to recklessness with regard to their weapon's discharge?

Finally, there can be no peace or insurance of the general welfare without the banning of semiautomatic guns, assault rifles, high-capacity magazines, bump stocks and any other device that creates machine gun-like capability or could be considered a military-grade weapon.

To this, perhaps, could be added an optional buy-back program on such currently owned weapons, or special use permits limited to certified firing ranges, where ammo distribution is strictly monitored and only used on-site.

Without such protections, or comparable ones, we are not safe, our children are not safe and the Nation is not safe. Claims of universal gun rights that fail to support our predominant Constitutional rights to Justice and Liberty, first and foremost, are null and void.

Without such protections, the blessings of Liberty for the many are trampled by a select number of violations by a relative few;

Without such protections, there can be no Tranquility for ourselves or our Posterity.

CHAPTER 4

§

THE BILL OF DEMOCRATIC RIGHTS

We the People of the United States, in Order to form a more perfect Union, vow to establish True Justice and Democracy, once and for All, through the fulfillment of our Words and Promises, and our most coveted Dreams, so long deferred, of those who came before.

It has been said in our initial Declaration that whenever any form of Government becomes destructive of these ends, it is the Right of the People to alter or abolish it, and to institute new Government, laying its foundation on such principles and organizing its powers in such form, in whatever way will best affect their lives and enshrine their liberties.

So after a long train of abuses, corruption, nepotism and despotism, it is now that time to embrace the right and duty of the People to throw off such Government and to provide new protections for our future security.

To this we add our New Words and Vows, toward the completion of our Republic, in keeping with the spirit in which it was conceived.

We seek to reinsure domestic Tranquility. We seek to provide, as always, for the common defense, not just for ourselves, but also for our Environment; let there not be dominion over Nature, but service to and alignment with her. And let our common defense also be against brutality in all shapes and forms. We seek to promote the general Welfare, not simply for property owners of the upper class, but for all classes of Americans.

We are older now. We can do better. We have another 250 years of our history to draw from, and learnings to put to use. The bar is higher, but we can, we must, we will rise to the task.

We continue to seek the Blessings of Liberty, for ourselves, our neighbors, our fellow citizens, and our posterity. We do hereby commit to the reestablishment of government, as dictated by our Constitution, its Amendments and this Bill of Democratic Rights. These must not be mere incremental or token changes, but a momentous change driven by great urgency and the will of the People.

We are reminded that Governments are instituted among Men and derive their powers from the consent of the People — not the other way around.

Democratic governments exist to ensure certain unalienable Rights, among these are Life, Liberty and the pursuit of Happiness. We reaffirm that these Truths must now finally be fulfilled: that all men are truly created equal — and that this is not just backed up with words, but by actionable and measureable deeds.

We, therefore, the People of the United States, appealing to the greater goodness of Humanity, do publish and declare these Democratic Rights, for the perfection and protection of the Union for which we stand.

AMENDMENT 28. — Transparency

Section 1. Transparency of government information shall be made and enforced to the full extent of the law, applicable to all federal employees — as this is, ultimately, the People's information.

Section 2. Communications of government officials in all branches of government shall be documented during their time in office and open to review upon request.

Section 3. Transparency of the executive branch, at the request of Congress, is of particular importance, including all requested records and communications before and during time in office, as a prerequisite to serving and remaining in office.

Section 4. Exceptions for governmental transparency can only be made in cases of national security, or in accordance with whistleblower protections.

Section 5. Policies and requests related to transparency in government shall be determined by a special congressional Transparency Committee, inclusive of civilian representation and oversight.

AMENDMENT 29. — Rule of Law

Section 1. The rule of law shall be clarified and codified across federal, state and local governments, wherever vagueness resides — making any informal or implied guidelines and traditions into explicit or enumerated laws.

Section 2. The rule of law shall be made tightly enforceable, and all governmental personnel held accountable, with clear penalties, to provide for proper checks and balances against the private power and corruption of those in positions of power and influence.

Section 3. No person in any branch of government may claim immunity for misconduct in relation to the rule of law. Misconduct shall be deemed a felony offense.

Section 4. The rule of law shall extend beyond the legal reach of individual administrations, for the consistent application of justice and order.

AMENDMENT 30. — Taxation

Taxation shall be reformed and simplified as follows:

Section 1. [1] No individual taxpayer form may be longer than a single page. Explanatory pages shall be no longer than three pages.

[2] The number of tax forms shall be no more than one.

[3] If these new standards cannot be met, then the government shall calculate and notify each taxpayer what they owe.

Section 2. The individual minimum amount that all

US citizens must pay shall be 10% of their adjusted gross income. No exceptions, no loopholes, except for those earning $20,000 or less (adjusted for inflation), who will owe $0.

Section 3. [1] The corporate minimum tax that all US corporations must pay shall be 20% of their effective tax rate based on their gross income. There shall be no exceptions, either through domestic, international, offshore havens, or any other loopholes.

Section 4. The annual individual income tax total paid toward the federal budget shall not exceed the annual corporate income tax total paid toward the federal budget.

AMENDMENT 31. — Education

Education, as a fundamental key to a successful America, with an intelligent electorate and equitable opportunity for all citizens, shall be expanded through new laws as follows:

Section 1. [1] Four years of public university education shall be made tuition-free for all Americans.

[2] Preschool education shall be provided tuition-free for all American families.

Section 2. Funding shall be provided for by the removal of tax loopholes.

AMENDMENT 32. — National Service

A National Service Corps program shall be created and executed, to share the load of service to the country, as follows:

Section 1. The National Service Corps will be created for the purpose of mandatory federal service in one of the military or civilian branches, including but not limited to: Army, Navy, Air and Space Force, Marine Corps, Coast Guard, National Guard, AmeriCorps, Peace Corps, Infrastructure Corps, Science Corps, Technology Corps and Teacher Corps.

Section 2. All American citizens between the ages of 18 to 25 years old must serve a term of 1 year of service.

Section 3. Funding will be provided for by the removal of tax loopholes.

AMENDMENT 33. — Campaign Finance

Section 1. Campaign finance shall be reformed shall be reformed as follows:

[1] Each candidate for President or Congress shall receive the same flat amount for their campaign ($100,000 maximum for Congress; $500,000 maximum for President).

[2] Each candidate shall receive equal minutes of airtime across public broadcasting systems in the three months prior to any election. No candidate may receive nor raise other funds, or broadcast ads privately, under penalty of disqualification.

[3] Political action committees shall be abolished.

[4] Unsanctioned advertising shall constitute a felony.

Section 2. All such campaign finance reforms shall apply to local, state and national elections. State and local maximum campaign funds shall be determined and allocated by those jurisdictions, but may not exceed standard levels common to all states.

Section 3. Funding related to campaign finance reform shall be provided by the removal of tax loopholes.

AMENDMENT 34. — Debts & Deficits

Section 1. [1] A balanced budget and a reasonable national debt shall be mandatory, for the purpose of sound fiscal policy, as stewards of the People's money and other assets.

[2] The executive and legislative branches shall work together to ensure that all budget income and expenditures are balanced every year, with Congress retaining the final say.

[3] A budget report, The U.S. Government Annual Report, shall be sent to all Americans annually. The section covering

budgets, debts and deficits shall not exceed three (3) pages.

Section 2. Congress shall have three (3) years to reduce the national debt such that it does not exceed the standard 60% of government debt-to-GDP.

Section 3. Congress shall have three (3) years to reduce the trade deficit such that it does not exceed the standard current account balance (CAB) of -100,000 (in million US dollars).

AMENDMENT 35. — Political Parties

Section 1. Political Parties shall, for the growth and health of the Republic, be expanded to include no less than five political parties.

If Section 5 of the Voting Amendment is not passed, then the following shall be made into law:

[1] A new Progressive party shall represent the more progressive and "left"-leaning aspects of the Democratic Party.

[2] A new Regressive party shall represent the more regressive and "right"-leaning aspects of the Republican Party.

[3] A new Independent party shall officially represent those who do not align with any of the other four parties.

Section 2. Beginning after the mid-term elections in November, 2022, the new parties will commence, with the intent to expand political power to better represent the voice of the People and to increase voter turnout.

Section 3. All parties shall be constructed such that they must form coalitions by interdependently working together in Congress. No-confidence votes by 2/3rds of all members may remove one ruling congressional coalition government from power at any point if they are deemed to have failed to govern competently.

AMENDMENT 36. — Healthcare

Healthcare will be reformed as follows.

Section 1. The People shall receive either the same or better healthcare options than their Senators, members of Congress, President and Justices, or they may select Universal Medicare for all.

AMENDMENT 37. — Local Defense

Section 1. Our nation's Local Defense — all police precincts — shall be audited and reformed nationwide, making all budgetary and disciplinary items subject to public knowledge and oversight, in perpetuity, as created through a special congressional Police Reform Committee in the House of Representatives, which researches, proposes, legislates and implements the top reform proposals, inclusive of a majority of public representatives specially chosen by professional peers for oversight.

Section 2. Reform methods will include but are not limited to: substantial defunding of police departments and/or unions, transfer of funding to education-based community programs, reduction of the scope and responsibilities of police duties, and demilitarization of police equipment.

Section 3. Police academy training of new recruits shall be no less than that of other major trades: a minimum of 2 years (currently, about 2-6 months).

AMENDMENT 38. — National Defense

Section 1. Our nation's National Defense — the Military and its affiliate structures — shall be reformed as follows:

[1] Military spending shall be reduced to no more than 25% of our discretionary budget spending (currently 54%), or no more than 33% below our total military budget (currently $950 billion, which is discretionary plus all other related branches or departments, such as the Department of Defense, Homeland Security, and the FBI), whichever is the

greater reduction. All amounts adjusted for inflation.

[2] Military spending shall be made as concise and transparent as possible to the public via The U.S. Government Annual Report, unless certain details are a matter of national security (as determined by an oversight committee). The report section covering military expenditures shall not exceed two (2) pages.

AMENDMENT 39. — Environment

Section 1. Our natural resources — land, air & water, and the creatures in it — are sacrosanct, and any attempt to limit reasonable environmental protections are punishable as a felony or with removal from federal office.

[1] International environmental laws, including standards set by a consensus of United Nations scientists representing a majority of countries, supersede the jurisdiction of individual administrations and shall not be violated.

[2] Any violations to these agreed-upon Environmental protections shall be subject to boycott and other severe penalties, economic and otherwise, as determined by the United Nations' International Court of Justice.

AMENDMENT 40. — Immigration

A firm immigration policy is necessary for a nation that prides itself both on a history of immigration and order by laws. Guidelines and protections, according to principles that transcend the vicissitudes and politics of individual administrations, are as follows:

Section 1. [1] Adopt the "Canadian system" as our base primary policy, which is a multi-point, merit-based evaluation.

[2] Make the family-based system a secondary priority.

[3] Maintain a minimum 18% rate of foreign-born citizens (currently 14%).

[4] Clarify and update the temporary worker system policy

so as to allow for an adequate supply of workers with temporary visas, to reduce and control the number of future undocumented workers.

[5] Increase new immigration to 2 million per year (currently 750,000), which includes the phasing-in of 20% per year of current DACA waitlist applicants, and 5% per year of current Undocumented Worker applicants, and allowing for a reasonable number of refugee and other applicants with regard to the remaining immigration slots per year.

AMENDMENT 41. – Voting

All voting systems and structures – local, state and national – shall be reformed and monitored to ensure voting is equitable for all citizens. The following shall be executed under new law:

Section 1. [1] The federal government shall be required to register all citizens to vote, cross-referenced by national population databases, IRS databases, and motor vehicle registration databases.

[2] State governments shall supply each voter with a mail-in ballot, or a voter may choose to vote in person.

Section 2. Voting reforms shall be instituted and monitored in the following manner, including but not limited to:

[1] Any attempts to restrict or inhibit easy voting shall be considered a felony crime, with immunity for none. This includes but is not limited to: gerrymandering, the limiting of voting locations, efforts to slander or limit mail-in voting or any other official method of voting, interference with the postal system to control mail-in voting, excessive voter ID regulations, attempts to prevent early voting, and mass purges of voting rolls.

[2] Gerrymandering shall be abolished. Voting districts shall be determined by the most equitable federally determined algorithm that is agreeable by vote to 2/3rds of both houses of Congress.

[3] Any laws related to the above methods that currently exist but are not being enforced shall be codified, with stricter penalties clarified.

Section 3. Voting ease and expediency shall be instituted in the following manner, including but not limited to the following:

[1] Voting shall be made as easy as possible, utilizing: universal mail-in voting, the option for in-person voting, motor-voter registration, and any other strategies that may increase ease of voting.

[2] All voters shall be given the means to vote starting one (1) month prior to any election.

[3] There shall be enough voting centers, fairly distributed and open three (3) days per week, that all voters must be able to cast their votes within thirty (30) minutes upon arrival at a voting center or through their chosen means of voting.

[4] Voting Day shall be moved to the first Saturday of November to ensure maximum turnout.

[5] No political campaign shall last longer than three months.

Section 4. Voting penalties shall be created and executed as follows:

[1] Proof of voting must be shown with the submittal of annual taxes or a penalty of .05% of an individual's adjusted gross income shall be applied to that individual's taxes. Alternatively, a night in jail may be served.

Section 5. Voting systems and structures shall be federally adjusted and instituted as follows:

[1] Ranked Choice Voting ("final-five") shall replace closed party primaries with open, nonpartisan primaries in which the top five finishers advance to the general election.

[2] Ranked Choice Voting ("final-five") shall replace plurality voting in the general elections, to decrease rancor of

political faction and encourage the healthy participation of more than two parties.

[3] The Electoral College, being in conflict with the "one person, one vote" provision of the Constitution, shall be abolished.

Section 6. [1] Congress shall update the 1965 Voting Rights Act, renaming it the John Lewis 2020 Voting Rights Act.

[2] The House of Representatives shall reconcile the Voting Rights Act with new proposals that broaden and protect the rights of all voters.

Section 7. [1] All residents of Washington D.C. shall receive their rightful representation of two (2) Senators and the appropriate apportionment of House of Representatives members relative to the most recent census population figures.

AMENDMENT 42. — Firearms

Section 1. Gun control regulations, as reasonable deterrents to violent crime, shall be as follows:

[1] Mandatory universal background checks, prohibiting purchases to those with serious mental health disabilities, convictions for violent crime, or a history of domestic violence, shall be federally mandated in cooperation with the states.

[2] A 10-day "cooling off" period is placed on all firearm purchases.

[3] State permits shall be required for firearms purchases, with proof of residency and sales only through a licensed state dealer (no gun show loopholes). Each state shall keep a registry of all firearm sales and transfers, cross-checked with federal records.

[4] Proof of completion of a thorough firearms training course is required for all firearms purchases.

[5] Mandatory gun insurance, with proof of secure storage

capability for firearms, is required, and gun owners are subject to liability litigation with regard to their weapon's discharge.

[6] There shall be no restrictions on funding studies about guns, gun violence, and healthcare topics related to firearm use.

[7] There shall be a ban on all semiautomatic guns, assault rifles, and high-capacity magazines, bump stocks and any other device that creates machine gun-like capability or could be considered military-grade weapons.

[8] There shall be an optional buy-back on newly banned firearms.

[9] A limited number of special-use permits for firearms collectors shall be provided, but those firearms shall be limited to certified firing ranges, where ammo distribution is strictly monitored and only used on-site.

AMENDMENT 43. — House of Representatives

The House of Representatives shall be reformed as follows:

Section 1. [1] Former Constitutional powers regarding trade and war shall be re-established in favor of the House of Representatives.

[2] Filibusters and all other techniques of obstruction shall be abolished, in favor of designated time limits.

Section 2. Extra duties and powers shall be given to the House, including:

[1] The authority and obligation to enforce all voting-related laws and amendments created to ensure equal democratic voting opportunities for all citizens, in keeping with the Voting amendment.

[2] The authority and obligation to balance the budget and reduce the deficit, except under extraordinary economic or emergency circumstances, in keeping with the Debts & Deficits amendment.

[3] The authority and obligation to update and monitor all tax-related laws according the Taxation amendment.

[4] The authority and obligation to ensure that proper Pre-K through College education is available to all citizens, in keeping with the Education amendment.

[5] The authority and obligation to ensure that proper healthcare is available to all citizens, in keeping with the Healthcare amendment.

[6] The authority and obligation to ensure that America has a clear and effective, updated immigration policy, in sync with the Immigration amendment.

[7] The authority and obligation to ensure that America has clear and effective Environmental laws and policies, and that those policies are in sync with world standards of the United Nations.

[8] The authority and obligation to ensure that American government is as transparent as possible, in keeping with the Transparency amendment.

Section 3. Preparation, publication and distribution of The U.S. Government Annual Report, sent to all citizens annually.

Section 4. Term, pay and age limits of elected officials shall be reformed as follows:

[1] Instead of an infinite number of 2-year terms, House of Representatives members shall be eligible for no more than three terms of three years each (9 years maximum).

[2] No House of Representatives member shall serve past the age of 70.

AMENDMENT 44. – Senate

The Senate shall be reformed as follows:

Section 1. [1] To create proper apportionment, representation shall become proportional with regard to the populations of each state. Up to 2 million citizens, a state shall receive 2

Senators; for each additional 2 million citizens a state has, that state shall receive 2 more Senators.

[2] The Senate shall not withhold hearings and voting on nominations of candidates to the Judiciary.

[3] Filibusters and all other techniques of obstruction shall be abolished, in favor of designated time limits.

Section 2. Term, pay and age limits of elected officials shall be reformed as follows:

[1] Instead of an infinite number of 6-year terms, Senators shall serve no more than two five-year terms (10 years maximum).

[2] No Senator shall serve past the age of 70.

AMENDMENT 45. — Executive

Executive powers shall be reformed as follows:

Section 1. [1] The president's formal and informal duties shall be further defined and shall strictly adhere to the rule of law, under penalty of censure.

[2] The president and members of the executive branch, or any other department or agency of government, shall not refuse congressional subpoenas, under penalty of removal from office.

Section 2. Limits on executive power include but are not limited to:

[1] Independent counsels that investigate the president or anyone in the executive branch shall operate outside of the jurisdiction of the executive branch, free of the dangers of being fired or replaced by a corrupt executive and administration.

[2] The Attorney General, or any other representative of the President, shall not have the power to fire or inhibit the duties of any other subordinate attorney general investigating the president or any branch of government. Subordinate AGs shall operate independently, outside of the jurisdiction

of the executive branch, except by majority vote in both chambers of Congress.

Section 3. [1] The president shall not primarily declare war – that authority is reserved for Congress, under duties assigned by the Constitution.

[2] The president shall not primarily determine trade agreements – that authority is reserved for Congress, under duties assigned by the Constitution.

Section 4. [1] All national militia used by a President shall be clearly marked as such, and with individual identification on each uniform, and may not be deployed without the use of body cameras. All body camera footage must be made public upon request.

[2] The President shall not retain or use personal staff that have not been approved by Congress.

[3] Whistleblowing procedures shall be strengthened so as to better protect their identity.

Section 5. [1] Only ½ of both houses of Congress's approval of a new bill shall be required to override the executive veto (currently, this is 2/3rds).

Section 6. Term, pay and age limits of elected officials shall be reformed as follows:

[1] The President's term(s) shall remain unchanged at four years (8 years maximum).

[2] No President shall serve past the age of 70.

AMENDMENT 46. – Judicial

Section 1. Judicial powers shall be reformed as follows:

[1] The number of Supreme Court justices shall increase to 15, to ensure a more equitable court.

[2] The federal nomination of all court judges, both Supreme Court and all inferior courts, shall be determined

by a merit-based recommendation system of legal peers, with citizen oversight.

[3] After peer-recommendations are completed, all nominees must receive 2/3rds approval by both the Senate and the House. If no threshold is reached after three candidates have been voted on, then the candidate with the most votes shall be chosen.

Section 2. Term, pay and age limits of elected officials shall be reformed as follows:

[1] Instead of lifetime terms, justices shall serve terms of no more than 15 years.

[2] No Justice shall serve past the age of 75.

AMENDMENT 47. — Constitutional Convention

Section 1. The House of Representatives shall convene a Constitutional Convention every twenty (20) years, for the regular review and systematic improvement of our government through the process of amendments and any other means deemed necessary toward the fulfillment of our Founders' promises for true democracy and a more perfect Union.

[1] House of Representatives members shall each receive one vote.

[2] Senators shall each receive one vote.

[3] To be reminded of our roots, the convention shall take place in Philadelphia, commencing on the 4th of July and culminating on September 17th.

CHAPTER 5

§

What more can be said for the sake of our Nation than a simple wish, a humble hope, that the future not forsake this experiment in Democracy at this crucial time of need.

Let us lean into these winds of change and finally create a Nation not conceived in mere words and empty promises, but made manifest in deeds and momentous achievement, through the rekindled will of a great Nation.

If there is indeed virtue to boldness, then we would do well to seize the time before it passes, not allowing indecision to leave us mired in the inertia of inaction and paralysis.

We would do well to cease our moaning and lamenting, and instead engage, bringing to bear our best angels, to pick up where the Providence of our loftier history last left off.

We would do well to recommit, in earnest, to these elemental Truths that sometimes, with Fortune's blessings, guide and turn the fates, bringing all manner of allies and forces to one's aid in the quest for Justice.

We would do well not to loiter in the shadows of the past but to shine a light on the darkness, bringing forth a transcendent vision of Truth, of Country: our aims, our potential, our future.

The trees of Liberty and Democracy are not endowed with guarantees of survival, but rather inclinations of Nature that we must nurture and prune, again and again, that they may continue to grow in their determined manners, and flourish to their full potential.

The Republic to which we stand, cannot long stand the corruption to which it is now subjected, for though we are strong in standing watch to outside forces, are we strong enough to thwart the rot from within?

But if there is comfort, it is in the commonality of Americans who yet share a love of decency, despite shades of difference. So many see the dire need to come together for the sake of the Nation and unite with one heart, one mind, one body and soul — to be knit together as one, as a whole People again. These are the perennial patriots who are unwilling to allow the slow undoing of the ultimate rights to which our Union has always been committed and to which it yet aspires.

If there is hope, it is that in our earliest writings it is said that governments derive their powers from the consent of the governed, not vice versa.

If there is hope, it is in the unfinished work, the unfulfilled Promises, the Dreams deferred, that all point true north, directly to those who fought for Liberty — let us not rest until we have ensured that they did not die in vain. So let them haunt us, and let them also grant us the courage, resolve and understanding that there can be no alternative but the success of this hallowed work.

If there is hope, it is in the constant reminders of our sacred obligation to noble pursuits, for which these times invite us to respond, calling forth the spirits of our founders. All freedoms now call to us for their completion, the basic things which we do require, to one day sing them loud and proud, with renewed meaning, that the words have been fulfilled.

If there is hope, it is in Equality of opportunity, so long out of reach yet coming slowly into focus. The tempering of greed and the destruction of special privilege is within our reach, if we could but convince ourselves to act to the fullest extent of our means. How long must we wait to leverage and seize the full weight of the People's innate power?

If there is hope, it is that life itself, at its best, is full of trials and tribulations, and that by meeting strife head-on we embrace challenging yet fulfilling lives, just causes and good trouble. May we be blessed with the task of battling to uphold righteousness and high ideals, yet ground them in practical methods and strategic goals.

If there is hope, it is in the patterns and principles of the universe which do build in seemingly eternal frustration and tragedy, only to speed up the days of reckoning, when the wheels of justice grind, and change comes, and the People stream out into the streets, joyous, disbelieving that Freedom would ever come at all.

If there is a hope, let it be in these new generations of brilliant and eager young minds, those who have already lived a lifetime in their youth and will not be satisfied to inherit and lead a Nation steeped in narrow-minded views. It is they who are now summoned to receive the torch of Liberty, to carry forth and forge a wholly new America. It is they who prepare to combat the common enemies of tyranny, disease, poverty, corruption and war. These generations are thrust upon the stage of history, to defend our Nation in this hour of need. The devotion they bring to this struggle will herald the emergence of a new and better America, once again a beacon to the world.

May this workshop in self-government become at long last self-realized, blossoming into a most precious flower, releasing the scents of Peace and Tranquility throughout the land, from sea to sea.

May the Dreams be fulfilled at long last, and visited upon All People, for All Time, completing the Promises of our Founders, the Dream for which they fought and for which we will always fight.

George Rolland Wolfe

ENDNOTES

1. Paine, Thomas. *The American Crisis. Philadelphia. December 19, 1776.*

2. Paine, Thomas. *Common Sense, February, 1776.*

3. Jefferson, Thomas. *Letter to William Stephens Smith, son-in-law of John Adams. November 13, 1787.*

4. Adams, Samuel. *"The Writings of Samuel Adams: 1770-1773" Samuel Adams. 1906.*

5. King, Martin Luther, Jr.

6. Ibid.

7. Madison, James.

8. https://repository.law.umich.edu/articles/452/

9. Paine, Thomas. *The American Crisis. Philadelphia. December 19, 1776.*

10. https://www.se.edu/native-american/wp-content/uploads/sites/49/2019/09/A-NAS-2017-Proceedings-Smith.pdf

11. Eisenhower, Dwight D. *Farewell Address. January 17, 1961.*

12. Ibid.

13. Meacham, Jon. *The Soul of America. Penguin Random House. 2018.*

14. MacLean, Nancy. *Democracy in Chains. Viking: Penguin Random House. 2017.*

15. Meacham, Jon. *The Soul of America. Penguin Random House. 2018.*

16. Pew Research Center. *FACTTANK: News in the numbers. May 14, 2019.*
    https://www.pewresearch.org/fact-tank/2019/05/14/more-than-half-of-countries-are-democratic/

17. https://www.mic.com/articles/118598/7-facts-from-the-around-the-world-show-how-absurd-americas-elections-really-are

18. https://www.brennancenter.org/our-work/research-reports/new-voting-restrictions-america

19. Reuters. *Southern U.S. states have closed 1,200 polling places in recent years. 9/9/19.*
    https://www.reuters.com/article/us-usa-election-locations/southern-us-states-have-closed-1200-polling-places-in-recent-years-rights-group-idUSKCN1VV09J

20. https://en.wikipedia.org/wiki/Gerrymandering

21. https://www.mic.com/articles/118598/7-facts-from-the-around-the-world-show-how-absurd-americas-elections-really-are

22. https://www.reuters.com/article/us-usa-court-voting/supreme-court-guts-key-part-of-landmark-voting-rights-act-idUSBRE95O0TU20130625

23. https://www.mic.com/articles/118598/7-facts-from-the-around-the-world-show-how-absurd-americas-elections-really-are

24. https://www.fec.gov/updates/statistical-summary-24-month-campaign-activity-2015-2016-election-cycle/

25. https://www.mic.com/articles/118598/7-facts-from-the-around-the-world-show-how-absurd-americas-elections-really-are

26. Ibid.

27. Kennedy, John F. *"Inaugural Address." Washington, D.C. January 20, 1961.* https://www.ushistory.org/documents/ask-not.htm. "Ask not what your country can do for you – ask what you can do for your country."

28. https://www.pbs.org/newshour/show/dreading-taxes-countries-show-us-theres-another-way

29. https://americansfortaxfairness.org/tax-fairness-briefing-booklet/fact-sheet-corporate-tax-rates/

30. https://www.epi.org/publication/ib364-corporate-tax-rates-and-economic-growth/

31. The Brookings Institute

32. https://www.investopedia.com/terms/d/debtgdpratio.asp

33. https://en.wikipedia.org/wiki/List_of_countries_by_current_account_balance

34. https://en.wikipedia.org/wiki/Balanced_budget_amendment

35. https://www.history.com/news/founding-fathers-political-parties-opinion
36. https://hbr.org/2020/07/fixing-u-s-politics
37. Scene on Radio podcast, Season 4. Duke University. Center for Documentary Studies. 2020
38. https://www.nationalreview.com/2018/09/states-key-to-senate-legitimacy/
39. https://www.washingtonpost.com/news/politics/wp/2017/11/28/by-2040-two-thirds-of-americans-will-be-represented-by-30-percent-of-the-senate/ Scene on Radio, Season 4.
40. https://wallethub.com/edu/how-much-is-your-vote-worth/7932/
41. Roosevelt, Teddy. "Lincoln and Free Speech." 1918.
42. Dred Scott v. Sanford (1857).
43. Buck v. Bell (1927).
44. The Civil Rights Cases (1883).
45. Plessy v. Ferguson (1896).
46. Hammer v. Dagenhart (1918).
47. Korematsu v. United States (1944).
48. Bowers v. Hardwick (1986).
49. Bush v. Gore (2000).
50. Exxon Shipping Co. v. Baker (2008).
51. Citizens United v. FEC (2010).
52. The Washington Post, 7/10/18.
53. https://www.businessinsider.com/most-powerful-militaries-in-the-world-ranked-2019-9
54. https://www.nationalpriorities.org/campaigns/military-spending-united-states/
55. https://www.marketwatch.com/story/this-is-how-much-it-will-cost-to-replace-the-tomahawks-used-in-syria-2017-04-07, https://en.wikipedia.org/wiki/Arleigh_Burke-class_destroyer
56. Eisenhower, Dwight D. Farewell Address. January 17, 1961.
57. https://en.wikipedia.org/wiki/Diseases_of_despair#:~:text=The%20number%20of%20deaths%20of,150%2C000%20per%20year%20in%202017.
58. Eisenhower, Dwight D. Farewell Address. January 17, 1961.
59. https://www.nytimes.com/2019/07/19/business/tuition-free-college.html
60. https://www.amtrak.com/content/dam/projects/dotcom/english/public/documents/corporate/testimony/2019/Amtrak-CEO-Anderson-House-T&I-Testimony-Feb-07-2019.pdf
61. https://www.politico.com/news/agenda/2020/04/16/the-right-way-to-bail-out-the-post-office-190271
62. https://www.epi.org/publication/its-time-for-an-ambitious-national-investment-in-americas-children/
63. https://www.pewresearch.org/fact-tank/2020/01/15/renewable-energy-is-growing-fast-in-the-u-s-but-fossil-fuels-still-dominate/, https://www.greenbiz.com/article/how-many-jobs-does-clean-energy-create, https://www.scientificamerican.com/article/would-a-green-new-deal-add-or-kill-jobs1/
64. https://thehill.com/blogs/congress-blog/healthcare/484301-22-studies-agree-medicare-for-all-saves-money
65. https://www.cnbc.com/2017/07/25/heres-how-much-members-of-congress-pay-for-their-health-insurance.html, https://www.verywellhealth.com/is-congress-exempt-from-obamacare-4107197
66. https://www.pewresearch.org/hispanic/interactives/u-s-unauthorized-immigrants-by-state/
67. https://www.pewresearch.org/fact-tank/2020/08/20/key-findings-about-u-s-immigrants/

ACKNOWLEDGMENTS

My sincerest thanks for editorial
assistance from: Thea Mercouffer,
Joe Rassulo, Zaha Wolfe,
Doug Vanesko and Boni Peluso.
Thanks to David Stewart for
his book design expertise.